William Shakespeare
A Very Peculiar History™

With added soliloquies

'He was not of an age, but for all time.'

Ben Jonson, playwright, 1572–1637

This book is for Teddy.
JM

Editor: Stephen Haynes
Illustrators: Jessica Palmer (cover),
David Antram, Mark Bergin, Penko Gelev,
John James, Nick Spender
Editorial assistants: Rob Walker, Mark Williams

Published in Great Britain in MMXII by
Book House, an imprint of
The Salariya Book Company Ltd
25 Marlborough Place, Brighton BN1 1UB
www.salariya.com
www.book-house.co.uk

HB ISBN-13: 978-1-908177-14-8

3 5 7 9 8 6 4 2
A CIP catalogue record for this book is available
from the British Library.
Printed and bound in India.
Printed on paper from sustainable sources.
Reprinted in MMXII

Visit our website at **www.book-house.co.uk**
or go to **www.salariya.com**
for **free** electronic versions of:
You Wouldn't Want to be an Egyptian Mummy!
You Wouldn't Want to be a Roman Gladiator!
You Wouldn't Want to be a Polar Explorer!
You Wouldn't Want to sail on a 19th-Century Whaling Ship!

Visit our **new** online shop at
shop.salariya.com
for great offers, gift ideas, all our new releases
and free postage and packaging.

William Shakespeare

A Very Peculiar History™

With added soliloquies

Written by
Jacqueline
Morley

Created and designed by
David
Salariya

'Shakespeare never had six lines
together without a fault. Perhaps
you may find seven, but this does not
refute my general assertion.'

Dr Samuel Johnson, writer and
lexicographer, 1709–1784

'I know not such a power
of vision, such a faculty of
thought,…in any other man. Such
a calmness of depth; placid joyous
strength; all things imaged in that
great soul of his so true and clear,
as in a tranquil unfathomable sea!'

Thomas Carlyle, historian, 1795–1881

'I have tried lately to read
Shakespeare and found it so dull
that it nauseated me.'

Charles Darwin, naturalist, 1809–1882

Contents

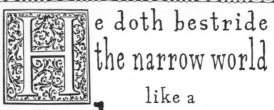

He doth bestride
the narrow world
like a

Colossus

Julius Caesar, *Act 1 scene 2*

INTRODUCTION

Who was Shakespeare, anyway?

hakespeare – what do you think of when you hear that name? Perhaps it brings back some great nights at the theatre, but, just as likely, it could make you think of a lacklustre school outing to a matinée, where enjoyment was compulsory and often subject to some 'class discussion' later.

Shakespeare, for most people, is something that is 'done' at school. But behind the name there is a real person, and, believe it or not, he wasn't always a balding man in a ruff. He was Mr and Mrs Shakespeare's boy, Will, who

grew up to make quite a name for himself. How did he do it? Where did he work? Why did he write, and how? Was he a nice person? What sort of friends did he have? This book doesn't promise neat answers to all those questions – that's often just not possible, as you'll see – but it's going to have a go at answering some of them. It will try to take a look at Shakespeare's work from Shakespeare's point of view.

Perhaps we'd better come clean here. Clear-cut facts, like where Shakespeare was on any particular day of the year, are certainly thin on the ground – not non-existent, but thin. Yet, even though they've been raked through so many times, by countless critics and historians, still there's no final agreement on exactly how much he wrote, when he wrote it, and what he did with his spare time.

But at the very least, we can dispose of some of the myths that have attached themselves to Shakespeare's name…

Shakespeare myth no. 1

So little is known about Shakespeare's life that you could write it down on one side of a postcard.

You'd need a quite extraordinarily big postcard, actually. There is more factual evidence about the life of Shakespeare than there is for any other Elizabethan dramatist. There are baptismal records, death and burial records, documents relating to the buying and selling of goods and properties, known performance dates for many of his works, and publication dates for poems and plays.

Many documents relating to the Shakespeare family, including letters written to William himself, can be seen at the Shakespeare Centre Library & Archive at Stratford upon Avon.

Speak of me as I am; nothing extenuate,
Nor set down ought in malice.

Othello, Act V scene 2

Queen
Elizabeth I

 pattern to all princes **living with her,** And all

that
shall **succeed**

Henry VIII, *Act V scene 5*

STRATFORD DAYS

 n 26 April 1564 the vicar of Holy Trinity Church, Stratford upon Avon, in the county of Warwickshire, recorded a baptism in his parish register: 'William, son of John Shakespeare'.[1] Will was the third of what were to be eight children, whose parents lived in a large house on Henley Street – where, 12 years earlier, John had been fined for not removing an illegal rubbish tip from in front of his door.

1. He actually wrote it in Latin: 'Gulielmus filius Johannes Shakspere'. (Though strictly speaking he ought to have written Johannis.*)*

John Shakespeare came from a family of local farmers, but a nose for business had prompted him to move from countryside to town, where he trained as a glover and soft-leather worker. He had obviously done well to be able to afford a substantial house in town.

Shakespeare myth no. 2

How fitting it is that England's greatest poet was born and died on 23 April – St George's Day, dedicated to England's patron saint.

Don't count on it – though he certainly *died* on 23 April. We know he was christened on the 26th, but we don't know his birthday. Babies were baptised as soon as possible, usually within five days, because it was believed that they came into the world in a state of original sin and were doomed to limbo if they died before baptism. This traditional Catholic belief was still strong despite England's official Protestantism – Henry VIII's break with Rome had come only 30 years earlier.

The five-day period gives William a birth date some time after 21 April. St George's Day was picked long after his death for patriotic reasons.

A worthy townsman

Stratford in 1564 was a small, prosperous market town of around 2,000 inhabitants. Its bridge over the Avon carried the route south to London, a three-day journey away.

John Shakespeare soon made his mark in the town as an entrepreneur. As well as dressing leather and selling gloves, he was a dealer in wool and farm produce. In fact he became quite a big splash in a not-so-small puddle. In 1558 he was sworn in as town constable, six years later he was made a burgess,[1] and in 1567 an alderman. He was twice elected town chamberlain, the official responsible for keeping the civic records and accounts, and then, in 1569, the final honour – he was chosen to be bailiff of Stratford (the equivalent of mayor).

On his father's side Will came from local yeoman[2] stock, rooted in the Warwickshire countryside. His mother's family, the Ardens,

1. *a member of the town council.*
2. *small-scale landowner.*

were more distinguished. They traced their ancestry back to Thorkell of Arden, a major landowner of Saxon times. Ardens had fought for Simon de Montfort, earl of Leicester, when he rebelled against King Henry III in the 13th century – and one of them was executed, a sure sign of distinction. A great-uncle of Will's mother, Mary Arden, had served at the court of Henry VII (reigned 1485–1509).

Though Mary was only distantly related to the grander side of the family, she bore its ancient name. The wooded area that covered much of Warwickshire to the northwest (enclosing the then insignificant town of Birmingham) was called the Forest of Arden. Many years later Will gave this name to a forest of his own imagining,[1] one of the many hints we get that his home town and the landscape of his childhood had a strong pull over him.

1. *in his comedy* As You Like It.

Shakespeare myth no. 3

He was brought up in an illiterate household – his parents couldn't read or write.

It's true that both John and Mary signed official documents with a mark, but that doesn't prove they weren't able to handle a pen. People well known to have been able to write sometimes did this. Since John was twice elected town treasurer, he must at the very least have been able to read and to count on his fingers.

England in 1564

When Will was born, Elizabeth I had been on the throne for five years. Most of her subjects were glad to see her there; they had been through rough times recently.

The Queen's father, Henry VIII, had made England Protestant because he couldn't get his way with the Pope. His son, Edward VI, was a convinced Protestant but his early death brought his Catholic sister Mary to the throne. She forced the nation to return to Catholicism – and protesters were burned alive. People must have held their breath when Protestant Elizabeth followed. But she was generally lenient with Catholics, who were fined rather than executed. Elizabeth's flair for compromise kept her people reasonably content for 45 years.

Will goes to school

At around the age of 5, young Shakespeare would have started at a 'petty' school (what we would call an infants' school). Here pupils were taught to read and write, to learn psalms by heart and to recite the answers to the Church catechism. At the age of 7 he went to Stratford's King Edward VI Grammar School for Boys. 'Not a shred of evidence that he did so,' say those who insist we know next to nothing about him (some of whom – see pages 175–176 – have a vested interest in suggesting he had barely any education at all). But it is almost inconceivable that he didn't. As the son of a burgess of the town he was guaranteed a free place. His father was on the committee responsible for the school's upkeep and for appointing its headmaster. So where else would William have gone?

The school was less than five minutes' walk away, in the large upper room of the Guildhouse. The corresponding ground-floor room was the local government headquarters. It also served as a temporary theatre when travelling players came to town.

Education was a tough business. William sat on a hard wooden bench from six or seven in the morning till five or six in the evening, with a short break for breakfast (bread and ale), home for lunch and back at one. Lessons were almost entirely a matter of studying Latin grammar and of translating, learning and repeating classical texts.

Boys of all ages studied together in one room. Yet the schooling was probably as good as any in England. The town council was enlightened enough to pay its teachers as much as the famous Eton College did. William studied with graduate teachers who seem to have been effective in making him familiar with the plays of Plautus and Terence, the writings of Cicero and the poems of Virgil, Horace, Ovid and Catullus. Pupils had to write fluently in Latin and to speak it too. Altogether, William's 'small Latin and less Greek', as rival playwright Ben Jonson dismissively put it, was probably more than the average classics graduate has today. This was the routine for six days out of seven. On Sunday Will attended morning and evening services – attendance was compulsory by law.

A first taste of the stage

School may have been a grind, but the regular round of country festivities brought plenty to look forward to: Twelfth Night, Shrovetide, harvest celebrations, and Stratford's home-grown festivity, the annual pageant of St George and the Dragon.

Just a few miles away at Coventry there was an even bigger show, the famous cycle of religious plays put on annually by the trade guilds for the festival of Corpus Christi. They formed a pageant, too. Each guild had its own scene which its members acted on its own little outdoor stage. It was an old tradition started by the medieval Church, but in the course of time the Bible stories had acquired all sorts of extras to amuse their audiences: comically horrible devils, rustic funny men, Herod madly rampaging, Noah's nagging wife. It may have been from visits to the Coventry plays that William got his love of spicing the most serious drama with sudden bursts of the earthy and comical.

Corpus Christi play:
the Devil and the mouth of Hell

Another great day was when the travelling players arrived in town. They were professional actors from London on a summer tour. Will must have often watched them parading down the street, sounding a drum and trumpet to let the town know they'd arrived.

Players could not perform without permission from the local mayor. During his time of office Will's father would have been the one to grant them leave to act in the Guildhouse and to invite the Stratford dignitaries to the first performance, which was known as the Mayor's Show. It's hard to believe that Will would have missed that play, or that he didn't wriggle in somehow to every one there was. And there were plenty of these visiting companies of players, often including some of the best actors in the country.

The companies

Like the Coventry plays, the travelling players were part of an old tradition, but a less respectable one: the tradition of the wandering clowns, jugglers, acrobats and musicians who performed in medieval streets. From the end of Roman times (in the 5th century AD) there had been no theatres or professionally acted plays. It wasn't till the 15th century that street entertainers began expanding their acts into fully fledged plays. The fact that they were called 'players' shows what most people thought of them – not much better than beggars, as they did no proper work.

Vagabonds who couldn't prove they had a master were harshly punished in Elizabethan England. They risked being whipped and branded. To get around this, a troupe of players would petition some nobleman to be its patron. He didn't pay the players but they were officially his 'men' (servants), belonging to his 'company' and kept to entertain him. The companies of the earls of Worcester, Leicester, Oxford and Derby, amongst others, visited Stratford while Will was a boy.

Out into the world

Stratford Grammar School equipped a student for university, but Will did not go down that route. Perhaps his father could not afford to send him – it seems he ran into quite a lot of debt in the late 1570s when there was a serious economic downturn in the Midlands. It's likely too that learning for its own sake had little appeal for him. In *Henry VI Part II* rebel leader Jack Cade threatens to execute one of the king's supporters because he has 'most traitorously corrupted the youth of the realm in erecting a grammar school'.

Whether it was his own idea, or prompted by the family's need for a second breadwinner (there were five children under 12 to support), William left school at around 14. This was the normal leaving age for boys who went into an apprenticeship. The natural place for Will to be apprenticed was with his father. This seems to be confirmed by the 17th-century biographer John Aubrey, famous for his none too accurate but entertainingly gossipy *Brief Lives* of notable people. Of 'Mr William Shakespeare' he records:

'His father was a butcher, and I have been told heretofore by some of the neighbours, that when he was a boy he exercised his father's trade, but when he kill'd a calf he would do it in a high style, and make a speech.'

Brothers and sisters

John and Mary had eight children – quite a modest head-count for the 16th century. Two baby girls died in infancy. Then came William, Joan, Gilbert, Anne, Richard and Edmund.

Anne died aged 8. The others made it to adulthood but little is known of them. Joan married a local hatter called William Hart. Gilbert seems to have followed his father's trade. Of Richard all we know is that he had some brush with the law in Stratford in 1606 and was fined 12 pence.

Edmund, the youngest, went to London and became an actor. Perhaps William, 16 years older, took him under his wing. There's no record of where he played, or in what, but in 1607 he was living in the Cripplegate area of London where the death of his infant son is registered. Six months later he was dead himself, aged 27. Someone paid 20 shillings for his funeral – a lavish outlay which surely must have come from his successful elder brother.

Only Joan outlived William – by 30 years.

The family man

The next news we have of Will, he's married – at the age of 18! There must be quite a story here, if only we knew. His bride, Anne Hathaway, was 26 at the time, and pregnant. She was a farmer's daughter from Shottery, a hamlet just a mile away. The Shakespeares knew her family well (some years before, John Shakespeare had helped to pay off a debt of her father's), so Will had known Anne since he was a child. They were married in November 1582. It was a rushed affair. The couple applied to the bishop's court at Worcester for a special licence to marry without the normal three weeks' delay of calling the banns. Whether Will saw it as happiness coming to meet him halfway, or whether Anne's father had to get out the shotgun, we'll never know.

Their daughter Susanna was born in May 1583, followed in 1585 by twins, Hamnet and Judith.[1] If the couple did the normal thing and moved into the Shakespeare home in Henley

---

1. *The twins were named after their godparents, Hamnet and Judith Sadler. The fact that 'Hamnet' sounds very like 'Hamlet' is just a coincidence.*

Street, Will may well have been feeling he had a lot of family on his back.

And then what happened? At this point we really don't know...

Shakespeare myth no. 4

He'd never meant to marry Anne Hathaway. He was already betrothed to a girl called Anne Whateley.

In the records of the Worcester court, the bride is named as Anna Whateley, described as a 'maiden' (virgin). But it seems this was just a case of a dozy clerk not keeping his mind on the job. There had been a legal case involving a Whateley earlier in the day and he confused the names – and didn't feel it was his job to look into the bride's condition.

Did Shakespeare join the army?

e go to gain **a little patch** of ground, That hath in it **no profit** but the name.

Hamlet, *Act IV scene 4*

CHAPTER TWO

THE LOST YEARS

he next time we hear of William, he's a well-known playwright with several hits to his name. That's in 1592. So what was he up to in those seven years between? There's no sign of him in Stratford.

Shakespeare scholars call this period his 'lost years'. They've been scratching around for centuries but they can't find what he did with them. That hasn't stopped people making plenty of suggestions:

1 He was escaping from an unsatisfactory marriage

There may be some truth in this. In a time when families were normally large (there was no reliable birth control), Will and Anne had no children after the twins. Maybe there were medical reasons, but a simpler explanation would be that Will just wasn't around to produce any.

It seems that at some time or other – we don't know why or when – he left Stratford. That doesn't prove he was a feckless husband and father; he may have left for the best of reasons. His father was getting elderly; Will, the oldest son, would feel responsible for the whole family. If he knew he had to be an actor or a writer, there was not much scope for him in Stratford. London was the place to make a name – and earn money to send home.

2 He'd fallen foul of a local grandee

This tale has been going the rounds since the 17th century. The story goes that Will was beaten and imprisoned for poaching deer from the country park of Sir Thomas Lucy of nearby Charlecote, and that he got his own back by writing a slanderous ballad about Sir Thomas and pinning it on the park gate. The knight was so infuriated, he took legal action that made Warwickshire too hot for Will.

Actually, it seems that there were no deer at Charlecote at the time. It's thought now that – if there's any grain of truth in the story – the falling-out could relate to something much more serious.

Sir Thomas was a fanatical Puritan and a great persecutor of Roman Catholics. There's evidence that Will's father was secretly faithful to the Catholic faith he was born into. Will's mother's family, the Ardens, certainly were. Sir Thomas had been the leading figure in a purge of local Catholics that brought one of the Ardens to the scaffold in 1583. If this was the source of the enmity between Sir

Thomas and the Shakespeare family, and if Will's ballad had anything to say on the matter, he could have been in real danger.

Catholic and Protestant

Elizabeth's first action as queen was to re-establish the Protestant Church after the reign of her Catholic sister Mary. By an act of 1559 she compelled everyone to attend Anglican services every Sunday. Those who refused were known as *recusants* (from the Latin *recusare*, 'to refuse'). They faced a fine or imprisonment. The majority of recusants were Catholics. Elizabeth's attitude to them was easy-going at first. She wanted a united people; she did not mind what they believed in private, so long as they went through the motions. But when Mary Queen of Scots, a Catholic claimant to the throne, became the focus of Catholic conspiracies, recusants faced harsher punishments and persecution began.

According to a profession of belief bearing his name (found in the 18th century hidden in the roof of the Henley Street house, but now lost), Will's father was a recusant. So the home Will grew up in was sympathetic to the old faith, on both his father's and his mother's side. Will gives us no hint as to how this affected him, though his eldest daughter was a firm and prominent Catholic all her life.

3 He joined a company of travelling players

Now this theory at least sounds plausible. Unfortunately there's no positive evidence for it. However, there is proof that a company of players that visited Stratford in 1587 had a vacancy.

This was the leading company of the day, the Queen's Men. Before coming to Stratford they were at Thame in Oxfordshire, where things got out of hand one evening, probably after some drinking. A witness saw one of the leading players, William Knell, brandishing a sword and chasing a fellow player, John Towne, around the close (courtyard) behind an inn.

According to the coroner's report:

'Towne, to save his life, drew his sword of iron (price five shillings) and held it in his right hand and thrust it into the neck of William Knell and made a mortal wound three inches deep and one inch wide.'[1]

1. 3 inches = 75 mm; one inch = 25 mm.

So the company arrived in Stratford one man short. It's a safe bet that if Will was in Stratford, he came to the play. But it's a long leap from that to supposing that a famous company would fill a gap in its ranks by recruiting someone with no training. The normal way into acting was through some form of apprenticeship.

4 He went to sea

This is one of the ideas people come up with through doing detective work on the texts. They have found lots of references to the sea and much use of nautical terms. Several plays involve a shipwreck; *The Tempest* has a spectacular one. The trouble with this line of reasoning is that it can equally well be made to show that Will was doing something entirely different, such as:

5 He was in the army

Any male over the age of 16 could be forcibly enlisted – and there are plenty of references to fighting in the plays! But again, no evidence.

6 He worked in a lawyer's office

This is the same theory at work. Legal terms abound in his work: 'summer's lease hath all too short a date,'[1] etc.

7 He was touring in Italy

There are lots of mentions of Italy in the plays, but that proves nothing. There are lots of mentions of Scotland, too! This idea is favoured by those who think he may have joined a troupe of wandering players. English companies toured abroad and were famous across Europe for their acting skills.

8 He went north, to Lancashire, and became a private tutor

This theory has had some critical backing recently, reinforced by the Shakespeare family's supposed Catholic sympathies. One of the masters at Will's school was from a Lancashire Catholic family and he could have got him a tutoring job up there. The evidence for this is a reference in the will of Alexander

1. Sonnet 18.

Hoghton, a prominent Lancashire Catholic, to a 'William Shakeshafte nowe dwellinge with me'. There are some holes in this argument (apart from the different name!). The will was made in 1581 when Shakespeare was 17. He can't have been in Hoghton's household very long, yet William Shakeshafte received a legacy of 40 shillings, a very large amount for a recent employee. The surname was not unusual in Lancashire: seven Shakeshafte households are recorded around this time, three with members called William. And how did Will have time to woo Anne and get her pregnant if he was already in Lancashire?

9 He went south, to London, and got into theatre work by minding people's horses while they watched the play

This theory at least has the merit of getting him where we know he ended up and of suggesting a not altogether unbelievable way of doing it. According to this legend he was such a reliable horse-minder that business expanded till he was employing several youngsters, who attracted patrons with the cry 'I am Shakespeare's boy, sir.'

Valet parking, Elizabethan style

This tale was set down in 1753 by the poet, playwright and actor Colley Cibber, who gave this account of its source:

Sir William Davenant [Shakespeare's godson] told it to Mr Betterton, who communicated it to Mr Rowe; Mr Rowe told it to Mr Pope and Mr Pope told it to Dr Newton, and from a gentleman who heard it from him 'tis here related.

Chinese whispers?

Of course, Will could have done more than one of these things. In seven years he might have done all of them! But unfortunately there is no proof that he did any of them.

Will Kempe dances from London to Norwich
(see page 48)

A fellow of infinite jest, of most excellent fancy

Hamlet, *Act V scene 1*

CHAPTER THREE

SETTLING IN

 e have to guess that it was some time in the late 1580s that Will arrived in London, perhaps lodging at a cheap inn at first, where he could get bed and food for a penny a night. What sort of city had he come to?

Old London Bridge

Shakespeare's London

As England's greatest port, with trade links that spanned the globe, London drew people like a magnet. With a population of over 200,000, it was bursting at the seams. Suburbs were spreading in all directions, far beyond the old city walls – eastwards beyond the Tower of London, westwards towards the court's elegant headquarters at Westminster, northwards into Shoreditch and southwards along the far bank of the Thames. Everywhere there was a mingling of fine houses and unregulated slums, as landlords threw up tenements on every patch of land, to house the influx of people swarming in to find a living.

London must have delighted Will and appalled him at the same time. It was known for its special smell, sniffable from afar – a rich mix of wood and sea-coal smoke from its forest of chimneys, of refuse from its street markets and open drains, and the whiff of numberless ceaselessly active bodies, sweating in heavy padded clothes. But it dazzled too. The sheer energy of it all! Cramped streets, humming with a thousand trades, opened onto thoroughfares lined with mansions and shops selling every kind of luxury. Hawkers shouted; ballad sellers sang their wares; inn yards spilled out laughter and tobacco smoke; crowds jostled everywhere. London was vibrantly alive and, above all, young (the high death rate, boosted by summer plagues, together with a constant influx of young hopefuls, saw to that). Life was short and Londoners snatched the most they could from it.

When Will arrived in London the main theatre district was in Shoreditch, beyond the city wall to the north. That was where theatre people, actors and playwrights, lived, so it was the natural place for him to look for lodgings and for work. There were two flourishing theatres there and people flooded out of the city to see their shows. Theatres – that is, buildings designed specifically for play-acting – were quite a recent idea. In the old days players had acted wherever they could, in market squares or inn yards or halls. They put up a makeshift stage on trestles, often in the open air, with a booth behind for changing in.

London inns had regularly hosted players. People packed into the open yard of the inn to watch, standing around the stage or looking down from the gallery that ran round the first floor. The plays drew great crowds, often very rowdy ones. There were constant complaints from local people about the noise – the drums and exploding fireworks – the congested streets and the drunken riffraff associated with them. The City authorities passed all sorts of restrictive laws to try to stop the nuisance of players using inns.

Travelling players in an inn yard

The Theatre

That was the position in the 1570s when the manager of the Earl of Leicester's Men, an enterprising man called James Burbage, came up with a bold idea. He rented some land at Shoreditch – which was outside the city walls, so London officialdom had no authority to stop him – and there he put up England's first purpose-built venue for plays. He named it 'The Theatre', from the Latin word *theatrum*,[1] presumably hoping that its association with ancient drama would give his venture a touch of class. He couldn't have known that he had invented the coming name for what the Elizabethans called a 'playhouse'. The Theatre opened in 1576 and was an instant success. Other people were quick to copy Burbage's idea. The Curtain playhouse opened just down the road in 1577. In 1587 the Rose was built south of London, across the river, followed by the Swan in 1595. Will's earliest plays were staged at the Theatre and the Curtain. What sort of building was he writing for?

---

1. *which comes from a Greek word that means 'a place for seeing'.*

James Burbage seems to have taken his idea from the bear-baiting rings, which were designed to cram in as many people as possible. Sad to say, many Elizabethans enjoyed the so-called sport of watching a chained bear being tormented by dogs. The enthusiastic crowds sat in tiered circles of seating in a round building with a central yard open to the sky. It had the advantage over an inn yard that the audience couldn't get in without paying, and it held far more people.

Bear-baiting

Burbage's building established the pattern for later Elizabethan theatres. It was a hollow circle. (Actually, being wooden, it wasn't truly round but made up of many short sides.) The seating could not extend all round, because on one side the stage and its changing booth stood against the wall. It was a trestle stage of the type the players had always used, but now permanently fixed and thrusting out into the yard so that the players were surrounded by the audience on three sides.

The changing booth, that used to be improvised with curtains, was now a wooden structure known as the 'tiring house',[1] two or three storeys high, providing backstage space for actors, costumes and props. Around 1,500 people could be seated in three tiers of galleries, and there was standing room for as many as could squash themselves into the open yard around the stage. There were plenty of rough types among these 'groundlings', as the standing audience was called, and a successful playwright had to grip their attention as well as pleasing the gentry in the seats.

1. Tiring *means 'dressing'; it's related to* attire.

Getting started

Will must have cut his teeth as a playwright by collaborating with other writers on patching up old plays and churning out new ones. That was how most plays were written then. Being a playwright wasn't anything great – it was hack work and poorly paid.

The demand for plays was huge. Theatre-going was such a new form of entertainment that there were simply not enough to go round. Companies performed six days a week, with a different play each day. A company could stage up to 40 different plays in a season, of which around 17 would be new.

As a jobbing co-author, Will must have been so much above the common level that he was soon asked to come up with his own plays. The first entirely written by him was probably *The Two Gentlemen of Verona* – but we don't know for sure which plays were written when, because no-one bothered to keep any records. The only reliable evidence we have is when the title of a play is mentioned in a surviving letter or memoir, or in a list of books for sale.

Dating Shakespeare's plays: an inexhaustible scholarly pastime

Critics look everywhere for clues: allusions in the plays to contemporary events, echoes of the dated works of other writers, the dates of printing (not necessarily the same as the date of writing), and developments in Shakespeare's writing style.

An Elizabethan schoolmaster called Francis Meres was particularly helpful. Writing in 1598, he compared Will favourably with ancient Roman playwrights, considering him 'among the English the most excellent in both kinds' (comedy and tragedy). Meres listed all of Shakespeare's plays to date, so from this we know which ones were written by 1598.

(The dates given in this Peculiar History are those suggested in *The Oxford Shakespeare: The Complete Works*, edited by Stanley Wells and Gary Taylor, revised edition, 2005.)

The Two Gentlemen of Verona heads Meres's list, which suggests it was the first to be staged. Critics agree that it shows signs of having been written by someone learning on the job.

The Two Gentlemen of Verona

c.1589~1590

This is a comedy with some disturbing emotional twists. The two gentlemen, Proteus and Valentine, are best friends. Valentine leaves to find fortune in Milan; Proteus prefers to stay in Verona with his beloved Julia. But when he too is despatched to Milan, he rapidly forgets Julia, falls for Valentine's love, Silvia, betrays his friend, and is only just prevented from forcing his attentions on Silvia in what amounts to attempted rape.

In the Spanish romance from which Shakespeare took the story, the death of the Silvia character enables the friends to be reconciled. But evidently Will needed a happy ending; he was writing to order, and that was probably what the company asked for. In an upbeat final scene that strains belief, all misdeeds are forgiven and the couples are abruptly paired off.

Comic relief is provided by Proteus's clownish servant, Launce, who comes on stage with a scruffy dog called Crab. He is devoted to Crab and gets nothing in return but ingratitude and embarrassment. In a running monologue he pours his heart out to the audience. Crab not only cocks his leg on ladies' farthingales but, not to put too fine a point on it, he farts a lot:

LAUNCE: He thrusts me himself into the company of three or four gentlemanlike dogs, under the Duke's table: he had not been there (bless the mark) a pissing while, but all the chamber smelt him. 'Out with the dog,' says one; 'What cur is that?' says another; 'Whip him out' says the third. 'Hang him up,' says the Duke.

I, having been acquainted with the smell before, knew it was Crab; and goes me to the fellow that whips the dogs: 'Friend,' quoth I, 'you mean to whip the dog?' 'Ay, marry,[1] do I,' quoth he. 'You do him the more wrong,' quoth I; ''twas I did the thing you wot[2] of.' He makes me no more ado but whips me out of the chamber. How many masters would do this for his servant?

Who is Silvia? What is she,
That all our swains commend her?

Act IV scene 2

This lyric is not one of the Bard's greatest, but is famous for having been set to music by Franz Schubert (1797–1828).

1. marry: *indeed (originally an oath sworn on the Virgin Mary).*
2. wot: *know.*

Will Kempe

Shakespeare created parts to suit the actors available. The garrulous servant Launce must have been tailor-made for Kempe, the most famous clown[1] of the day. He's known to have played the servant Peter in *Romeo and Juliet* and Constable Dogberry in *Much Ado about Nothing*, and though it's not recorded he must surely have created Bottom in a *A Midsummer Night's Dream*, Lancelot Gobbo in *The Merchant of Venice* and possibly Falstaff in *Henry IV*.

Kempe was small and stout but very nimble on his feet. He was famed for his dancing. In 1600 he made good a bet that he could do a morris-dance all the way from London to Norwich – a distance of around 100 miles (160 km). It took him nine days (not actually nine *consecutive* days) and was a triumph. Crowds flocked to watch him. When he reached Norwich the city gave him a pension and nailed up his dancing shoes in the Guildhall in memory of the feat. Kempe later published a detailed account of his 'Nine Days' Wonder'.

---

1. *In Shakespeare's day the word* clown *usually meant a country bumpkin.*

Heroines in disguise

The women are much nobler than their menfolk in *Two Gentlemen*. Faithful Julia decides to seek out Proteus and disguises herself as a man for safety's sake. A woman disguised as a man was a favourite ploy in plays of the time. Apart from its role in the plot, it was a sort of in-joke between the players and the audience. The female character pretending to be a man was, in reality, a man (or rather, a boy) dressed as a woman. There were no actresses on the Elizabethan stage – acting was not a very reputable way of earning a living, and women just didn't do it. This left a career opening for boys, who were trained to act the female roles. You can see how this ambiguous male/female situation – where a supposed man, who is actually a female character in disguise (and in real life a male actor), can be in love with another man – might allow actors to get quite a bit of sly innuendo out of their lines, in comedy at least.

Getting a toe in the stage door

Many actors began their careers at the age of 10 or 11 by being apprenticed to an established player, who trained them to play female roles. Just like apprentices in other trades, they got no pay during training, apart from food and lodging at their master's house. When they were skilled in the appropriate movement, gestures and voice production, their master would rent them to the company and – provided they showed acting promise – their career was launched.

It was a tough life with long hours. Until he was earning his master some money, an apprentice was put to work in other ways, running errands and doing chores. And, no matter how successful he became on stage, time was not on his side. When his voice broke and his chin grew bristly he would have to bow out. Only the most valued apprentices might hope to be kept on by the company for adult roles.

The Taming of the Shrew
c.1590

This early effort is a roaring comedy, based on the brutal but highly popular folk theme of how to clobber a bolshy wife. Male suprematist Petruchio unashamedly declares he is marrying shrewish Katherine for her money and will soon sort out her fiery temper. By means of hectoring and some pretty rough treatment, she has been transformed by the end of the play into a meek and totally obedient wife. Not a message to warm the hearts of 21st-century feminists – what was Will thinking of?

Well, he probably didn't give the plot two minutes' thought. A play with a similar title was already going the rounds at the time. Very likely Will was asked to improve it or to write a new version. Provided it worked on stage and kept the audience laughing, he had done his job. He created two punchy characters who generate enough sparks between them to allow plenty of different interpretations on stage, from knockabout farce to a feisty love story where instant attraction is masked as the battle of the sexes.

Will was soon trying his hand at one of the day's favourite entertainments: historical pageantry, with a strong appeal to patriotic sentiment.

The triple-decker we now call *Henry VI Parts I, II and III* (1590–1592), telling of the origins of the Wars of the Roses (not such distant history then),[1] was a popular success. However, success on the Elizabethan stage wasn't measured by the length of a play's run, as it is now. To keep afloat financially, Elizabethan theatres depended on getting more or less the same audience to come again and again, and for that they needed a different play each day. Plays that were well received were aired again later; 10 or 20 scattered performances amounted to a hit. Those that bombed weren't acted twice.

Henry VI Part I seems to have been a prequel to Parts II and III. The series made Will's name. Fellow playwright Thomas Nashe, who may have collaborated on Part I, told how packed theatres were moved to tears by the death of soldier-hero John Talbot.

1. *The wars ended in victory for the new Tudor dynasty in 1485.*

The plays in brief
Henry VI Parts I, II and III
1590~1592

The subject of these plays is the civil wars of the 15th century between the rival houses of York and Lancaster, whose emblems were the white and the red rose, respectively. Will took his historical facts from the chronicles of the contemporary historian Raphael Holinshed, who interpreted the turmoil of the previous century as the divinely ordained lead-up to the triumph of the Tudors. How much Will bought into this version of history is open to debate. It's true that the plays have a lot to say in favour of strong rule and against civil strife, but the main emphasis is on action-packed drama, with plenty of processions, battles, murders and a generous supply of severed heads.

Part I opens with the English nobles vying for control of the new king, the Lancastrian Henry VI, who is young and weak. The Duke of York plots to seize the throne. In London's Temple Garden the Yorkist and Lancastrian factions pluck their symbolic roses. Meanwhile the war in France is going badly. Joan of Arc features as Joan la Pucelle, a ferocious figure who defeats the French Dauphin (crown prince) in single combat and routs the English army by witchcraft. That was how she was seen in Tudor England!

> Damsel of France, I think
> I have you fast.
> Unchain your spirits now with
> spelling charms,
> And try if they can gain
> your liberty.

Part I, Act V scene 3

In *Part II* the struggle for France is over (England lost). The focus is now on infighting at home. While Henry dithers and the nobles bicker, the opportunistic Duke of York outmanoeuvres everyone.

The meek and holy Henry is out of step with the times, which are dangerous and bloody. 'What are you made of?' his truly horrific queen, Margaret of Anjou, demands savagely. (Remind you of anyone? Compare Lady Macbeth, page 130.)

Part III is one of Will's most violent plays. It shows a country in breakdown: fathers murder their own sons, and sons their fathers. York is captured by Margaret's forces. She mocks him with a paper crown and stabs him to death herself. Henry is finally murdered in his cell by York's son, Richard Duke of Gloucester – a hero-villain in waiting, to be met again in a later play (see pages 59–61).

The upstart crow

By 1592 Will was known in London's theatre world as the up-and-coming author of several successful plays. We know this because at least one writer was jealous enough to slate him publicly.

In a pamphlet of that year, playwright and general drop-out Robert Greene lampooned an unnamed writer by calling him an 'upstart Crow beautified with our feathers', someone who, 'with his tiger's heart wrapped in a player's hide, supposes he is as well able to bombast[1] out a blank verse[2] as the best of you: and being an absolute Johannes factotum,[3] is in his own conceit the only Shake-scene in a country.'

Greene is saying that Shake-scene is a jumped-up jack-of-all-trades (both actor and writer) who pinches other writers' plots and lines (quite true, but everyone did it and Will just did it better). Yet by parodying him

1. *bombast: pad.*
2. *blank verse: see pages 102–103.*
3. *Johannes factotum: literally, 'John do-all'.*

('O tiger's heart wrapped in a woman's hide!' – *Henry VI Part III*, Act I scene 4) he proves that Will's plays had made such a mark that a line from them was instantly recognisable.

Revenge, revenge!

History plays had been top audience-pullers for many years when Will hit town, but in the 1590s a new kind of drama was all the rage. The trend-setter was Thomas Kyd, whose *Spanish Tragedy*, a blood-spattered play of revenge, was the runaway success of the decade. Audiences couldn't get enough of gory revenge plots with details as gruesome as possible.

If this was what the punters wanted, Will was ready to show he could deliver – better than anyone. The result was *Titus Andronicus*, his first sensational hit – a revenge play of the first order, unashamedly tailored to the taste of the day.

Titus Andronicus

c.1593

Titus Andronicus provides not just blood, but buckets of it. The Roman general Titus and his four sons are involved in a drama of intrigue, murder, madness and cannibalism. The text includes the suggestive stage direction: 'Enter a messenger with two heads and a hand.'

The play has all the ingredients of a sure-fire success:

- 11 murders
- three people executed (one buried chest deep and left to starve)
- one rape with tongue and hand lopping
- two characters cooked in a pie and served to their mother.

The revenge craze didn't last much beyond Will's day. By 1678 *Titus* was being described as 'the most incorrect and indigested [*sic*] piece...rather a heap of rubbish then [*sic*] a structure'. The 20th-century poet T. S. Eliot called it 'one of the stupidest and most uninspired plays ever written'.

The plays in brief
The Comedy of Errors
1591~1594

This is a helter-skelter romp on a classical pattern, still hugely funny in a good production. It concerns identical twin brothers separated and unknown to each other since childhood, who have a second pair of separated identical twins as manservants.

Sounds far-fetched? That's nothing to the ludicrous antics Will puts them through by getting them to the same town (wearing identical clothes, of course), where the pairs are constantly mistaken for each other. He took the twins idea from an ancient Roman comedy by Plautus, who was a dab hand at neat plotting. But Plautus's play has only one set of twins. Will doubled the twins and quadrupled the mayhem.

Methinks you are my glass,
and not my brother.
I see by you I am a sweet-faced
youth.

Act V scene 1

Richard III
1592~1593

We now come to Will's first really outstanding character – one of his great villains, a ruthless schemer with an uncanny power to bend people to his will. He was already taking shape in Will's mind in *Henry VI Part III*, where he appears as Richard of Gloucester, already with that note of mockery in his voice:

Why, I can smile and murder whiles I smile...
Can I do this, and cannot get a crown?
Tut, were it further off I'd pluck it down.

This has more than an echo of the stock villain from the old guild plays. When it came to writing *Richard III* Will's increasing command of character and verse produced a more disturbingly wicked figure, counterfeiting total honesty while stepping back from his actions and enjoying the skill of his own performance. Richard glories in his wickedness and so does the audience. A character who is that good at being bad is great to see in action.

In pursuit of the crown Richard dupes his brother, Edward IV, into imprisoning their other brother, Clarence, whom Richard then has secretly killed. He lovingly ushers his young nephews (one is the boy heir) into the Tower of London on Edward's death. With breathtaking impudence he successfully woos the widow of a prince he's killed, over the coffin of her royal father-in-law, whom he's also killed. And she knows this!

Was ever woman in this humour woo'd?
Was ever woman in this humour won?
I'll have her – but I will not keep her long.

He's soon planning to murder her so that he can marry his niece. He declares his nephews illegitimate and gets himself crowned. Anyone who disputes his right is executed. The Princes in the Tower are liquidated. Everything is going Richard's way – except history. He can't escape being defeated in the last act by Richmond, the future Henry IV. During the night before the decisive battle he is visited by the ghosts of his victims – eleven of them. Not a bad score in the villainy stakes.

Now Will pulls off one of his great effects: when Richard wakes, his nerve is gone. The broken rhythms of the verse convey his frantic state of mind:

Cold fearful drops stand on my trembling
*   flesh.*
What do I fear? myself? there's none else by:
Richard loves Richard; that is, I am I.
Is there a murderer here? No – yes, I am:
Then fly? What, from myself? Great reason
*   why:*
Lest I revenge. What, myself upon myself?
Alack, I love myself. Wherefor? For any good

That I myself have done unto myself?
I shall despair. There is no creature loves me;
And if I die no soul shall pity me:
Nay, wherefore should they, since that I myself
Find in myself no pity to myself.

The audience gets a good battle scene to end with, and victorious Richmond ushers in a century of Tudor rule:

The day is ours, the bloody dog is dead...
We will unite the white rose and the red.[1]
Smile heaven upon this fair conjunction.

Now is the winter of our
discontent
Made glorious summer by this sun
of York.

Act I scene 1

A horse! A horse! My kingdom
for a horse!

Act V scene 4

1. the emblems of the houses of York and Lancaster, later combined to form the red and white Tudor rose.

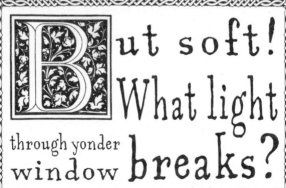

But soft! What light through yonder window breaks?

Romeo and Juliet, *Act II scene 2*

GETTING INTO HIS STRIDE

t's not clear what company Will worked for in the early days. Players chopped and changed, but by 1593 he seems to have been with the Earl of Pembroke's Men.

It was a bad year, not just for the players but for everyone. London was stricken by the deadly fever known as the plague. Every few years there was an outbreak, but this year was one of the worst. More than one in ten Londoners died.

The disease was spread by fleas from infected rats, but this wasn't understood at the time. However, people did notice that it was passed on rapidly in crowds, and in plague years the authorities closed the theatres as a precaution. They weren't allowed to reopen until plague deaths fell to fewer than 50 for three weeks running.

So between February 1593 and June 1594 there was no theatre work in London. Companies had to take to the road and tour the country. We can imagine Will travelling on a players' cart, or, if he could afford it, riding alongside (it was expensive to take a horse on tour). The Earl of Pembroke's Men did badly. By the summer they were out of work, and folded. Will had to find some other way of earning a living. Luckily he had something up his sleeve.

He must always have known that he had it in him to be a poet. Writing verse plays was not serious stuff, whereas poetry was highly regarded and the ability to appreciate it was the mark of a cultivated mind. Encouraging outstanding poetic talent with gifts of money was the recognised way for a nobleman to shine intellectually. So in the summer of 1593 Will published a long narrative poem, *Venus and Adonis*, with a preface dedicating it to the young Earl of Southampton.

The poem describes the overwhelming but frustrated passion of the goddess of love for the handsome youth Adonis. It is luscious, amorous and finally tragic; its first readers found it deliciously 'wanton' (titillating).

It was an immediate success, republished 11 times in the next 25 years, and did more for Will's reputation in his lifetime than any of his plays. The earl must have been pleased with the horse he'd backed, for next year Will dedicated a second narrative poem to him, *The Rape of Lucrece*, again on a classical theme. The tone of the dedication suggests that Will was now on cordial terms with his patron – and presumably getting well paid.

Later, when Will's stature as a serious poet was well established, publishers would put his name on the title pages of books he had little or nothing to do with, as a selling point.

The Passionate Pilgrim (1599) is one of these, though it has some verses filched from him. *The Phoenix and the Turtle* (1601), a collection by various authors about the legendary phoenix's love for a turtle dove, has just one poem attributed to Will. Scholars accept that it is his, though they continue to argue over 'A Lover's Complaint', which appeared in 1609 as an addition to his *Sonnets* (see page 157).

from hired man to sharer

Southampton may have been the source of funds that helped Will make a very sound investment at this time. So many companies were in difficulties after the plague year that the quality of Her Majesty's royal entertainment seemed in peril. In theory the players existed solely to entertain the court and the nobility. They were allowed to give other performances through the fiction that these were just 'rehearsals' – though audiences paid to see them.

In 1594 the Lord Chamberlain, Baron Hunsdon, straightened matters out by poaching the best players from various companies to form a new one, under his patronage, to be known as the Lord Chamberlain's Men.

Though a company took its name from its patron, it was owned and run by its 'sharers'. These were players who had invested money in the company and received a share of the takings. Other players only got a wage and were known as the 'hired men'. Among the eight named sharers of the newly formed Chamberlain's Men were Will Kempe, Richard Burbage (son of James who built the Theatre) and William Shakespeare.

The Chamberlain's Men became London's most successful acting company. Will stayed with it for the rest of his working life. Investing in it at the outset was an early sign of his sound business sense.

Shakespeare's rivals

The Chamberlain's Men's only significant rivals were the Admiral's Men at the Rose theatre, south of the river. Both companies had a strong leading actor and some great plays. (Companies owned the plays they'd commissioned, and didn't let the texts of successful ones out of their hands.) The Chamberlain's Men had Richard Burbage, an outstanding actor, and Shakespeare's plays. The Rose had the equally popular Edward Alleyn and the plays of Christopher 'Kit' Marlowe. Alleyn, over 6 feet (1.83 m) tall, was famous for the stalking walk with which he created Marlowe's towering hero Tamburlaine.

Kit Marlowe was top dramatist when Shakespeare came to town. He could write poetry that bowled audiences over with its swagger and rhythmic swing. Shakespeare fell under its spell and stole whole lines from him. Soon they were rivals and Marlowe was stealing from *him*. We can only guess who would have won in the end (the short odds are on Shakespeare), as Marlowe was murdered in a tavern brawl in 1593. He was only 29.

The plays in brief
Love's Labour's Lost
1594~1595

The best way to describe this is to say it's a 'wordy' play. That doesn't mean it's stodgy. On the contrary, its characters just love exchanging banter and scoring points off each other. They play games with words, as if Will was in love with words himself.

The play begins with the young King of Navarre and three of his lords vowing to take life more seriously in future. They will devote themselves to study for three years and renounce female company. But they have somehow forgotten that the Princess of France is due to arrive at any minute on a diplomatic mission. Very soon the King is in love with the Princess, and each of his nobles with one of her ladies.

All set for a happy ending? Not quite. At the end of this sparkly play a shadow falls. A messenger brings news that the Princess's father has died. The ladies hurry away, telling their suitors to stop playing at love and prove they're made of serious stuff by working for a year among the sick.

Will's way with words

Elizabethan English had no set rules. Use a foreign word if you fancy it, use a noun as a verb, stretch a word to carry a new meaning, put two together to make another, feel free to invent an entirely new one – Will did all of this, and many other writers did too. Some scholars got so word-drunk on recently rediscovered classical authors that they swamped their prose with Greek and Latin words. Will didn't care for that sort of affectation, and made fun of it in *Love's Labour's Lost*. The comic Spaniard Don Armado, described as 'a man of fire-new words', speaks of 'the posteriors of this day, which the rude multitude call the afternoon'. 'Fire-new', Will's shorthand for 'new as a blade fresh from the forge or a pot from the kiln',[1] is the sort of word-coinage he favoured – original but instantly understandable.

1. The term 'brand new' also originally referred to something hot from the fire – a brand is a piece of burning wood.

Shakespeare myth no. 5

Shakespeare invented a quarter of all the words in the English language.

Even if this means 'the language of his time', it's far from true. The *Oxford English Dictionary*, which gives the earliest date when a word appears in an English text, cites him as first user of around 2,200 words, which is nowhere near a quarter of the Elizabethan dictionary (if they'd had such a thing, which they didn't). And being the first user of a word doesn't prove he invented it, only that he was (as far as we know) the first to write it down.

However, it seems that up to 1,700 words *could* be his invention – the biggest score of any English writer. Some of them, such as *insultment*, *irregulous* and *exsufflicate* (puffed up), didn't catch on, but *assassination*, *courtship*, *outbreak*, *sanctimonious*, *fashionable*, *exposure* and *vulnerable* are just a few of the hundreds that did.

He coined some useful 'un-words' too: *uncomfortable*, *unearthly*, *uneducated*, *unmask*, *unveil*, *unlock* (though *unshout*, *undeaf* and *unbuild* weren't winners).

The plays in brief
Romeo and Juliet
1595~1596

After the rather brittle *Love's Labour's Lost*, Will explores much deeper feelings in the whirlwind tragedy of *Romeo and Juliet*. Its hero and heroine are innocents who fall in love instantly, marry almost immediately and have just one precious night together before their families' senseless feuding tears them apart. It's a play about what it feels like to be very young, when all emotions, even imaginary ones like Romeo's early crush on Rosalind, are overwhelming, and true love, when it comes, strikes like a thunderbolt – an experience almost beyond words to express. Yet Will can do it. Here is Juliet in torments of impatient love:

Come, night; come, Romeo; come, thou day in night;
For thou wilt lie upon the wings of night
Whiter than new snow on a raven's back.
Come, gentle night – come loving, black-brow'd night,
Give me my Romeo; and, when he shall die,
Take him and cut him out in little stars,
And he will make the face of heaven so fine
That all the world will be in love with night,
And pay no worship to the garish sun.

William Shakespeare

It's said that in *Romeo and Juliet* the part of Friar Lawrence was played by Shakespeare. It would be exaggerating to claim he was a major star, but at Christmas 1594, when the Chamberlain's Men played before the Queen at Greenwich Palace, payments of £20 each were made to three named players: Richard Burbage, William Kempe and William Shakespeare. So Shakespeare's acting was rated highly enough to put him in the top three.

He was acting for more than 20 years, and for most of that time he was with the best company in the land. To be of any use to them, he must have been able to sing, dance, fence nimbly, swing a sword convincingly and play a musical instrument. The idea that he was a mediocre actor doesn't crop up till the 18th century, when it was said that 'The top of his performance was the Ghost in his own *Hamlet*.' The 17th-century historian John Aubrey reported that 'He could act exceeding well.' He is said to have specialised in kingly roles. Will may have created the monarch in *Henry VI*, *King John* and *Henry IV*, and the duke in *A Midsummer Night's Dream*.

The plays in brief
Richard II
1594~1595

Will returned to history with *Richard II*. This
time he is less interested in history as an
unfolding pageant and more in the personal
tragedy of a weak and oversensitive man, quite
unsuited to rule. Richard is destroyed by the
usurper Bolingbroke (later Henry IV), who is
purposeful and strong. But Bolingbroke
figures in the play largely as the trigger to the
action – the interest is all on Richard, whose
self-dramatisation (he is a great poser) is
uttered in lyrical verse:

> *For God's sake let us sit upon the ground*
> *And tell sad stories of the death of kings.*
> *. . . for within the hollow crown*
> *That rounds the mortal temples of a king*
> *Keeps Death his court; and there the antick[1]*
>   *sits,*
> *Scoffing his state, and grinning at his pomp,*
> *Allowing him a breath, a little scene*
> *To monarchise, be feared and kill with looks;*
> *Infusing him with self and vain conceit,*
> *As if this flesh, which walls about our life,*
> *Were brass impregnable; and humour'd thus,*
> *Comes at the last, and with a little pin,*
> *Bores through his castle-wall, and –*
>   *farewell king!*

1. antick: joker, mocker.

What a chameleon Will was! He had only to set a fresh plot in motion for his language to take on a colour that belonged uniquely to that story and those characters. At one moment he is voicing the passion of *Romeo and Juliet* or the fretful anguish of *Richard II*, the next he is spinning the moonlit fairy comedy of *A Midsummer Night's Dream*.

If you only know one play of his, it's probably this one. It's popular with schools because it's not emotionally taxing and has such variety of character and incident that there's something to appeal to almost everyone – and almost everyone will get a part.

The course of true love never did run smooth.

A Midsummer Night's Dream, Act I scene 1

A Midsummer Night's Dream
1595~1596

Will was inspired by the Latin poet Ovid, a favourite from his schooldays, whose *Metamorphoses* (meaning 'Transformations') tells how the whims of the gods changed people into trees or flowers or other shapes.

But trust Will to complicate things for maximum effect. Ovid has one transformation per story; Will manages an accumulation of them. He takes some ill-assorted lovers from ancient Athens (Lysander and his sweetheart Hermia, who is fleeing a forced marriage to Demetrius, who is seeking her through the woods, pursued by his rejected love, Helena) and leads them into an unsettling fairy world where hearts and shapes are magically changed, and changed again.

On this midsummer night, the haughty fairy king Oberon and his queen Titania are having a mighty quarrel. The king plots revenge. While his queen sleeps he will smear her eyes with a herb that will make her fall in love with whatever she sees on waking:

OBERON: I know a bank where the wild thyme blows,
  Where oxlips and the nodding violet grows;
  Quite over-canopied with lush woodbine,

With sweet musk-roses and with eglantine,
There sleeps Titania sometime of the night,
Lull'd in these flowers with dances and
       delight;
And there the snake throws her enamelled
       skin,
Weed[1] wide enough to wrap a fairy in:
And with the juice of this I'll streak her eyes,
And make her full of hateful fantasies.

With a kinder motive he also orders his impish servant Puck to smear Demetrius's eyes, expecting he'll see Helena when he wakes and dote on her. But Puck mistakenly smears Lysander's eyes, making *him* love Helena. Correcting the mistake makes matters worse: this time he gets the right man, but, with both men unaccountably saying they adore her, Helena thinks they are making fun of her, while Hermia, now the forsaken one, flies at her in a jealous rage:

HERMIA: *O me! – you juggler! You canker*
       blossom!
  You thief of love! what, have you come by night
  And stol'n my love's heart from him?
HELENA: *O, when she's angry, she is keen and*
       shrewd!
  She was a vixen when she went to school;
  And though she be but little, she is fierce.
HERMIA: *'Little' again! nothing but 'low' and*
       'little'!
  Why will you suffer her to flout[2] me thus?

1. *Weed: garment.*   2. *flout: insult.*

Meanwhile, some clownish craftsmen have come to the woods to rehearse a play which they plan to act at the wedding of the Prince of Athens. Puck transforms the head of loud-mouthed Bottom the weaver into a donkey's, so that when Titania wakes she adores an ass-head and commands her fairies to attend him:

Feed him with apricocks and dewberries,
With purple grapes, green figs and
> *mulberries;*
...

And pluck the wings from painted butterflies,
To fan the moonbeams from his sleepy eyes...

But all the night's troubles are cured by fairy magic. By one last transformation Lysander's true feelings are restored, and next day all ends in good-natured laughter as the craftsmen blunder through 'the most lamentable comedy and most cruel death of Pyramus and Thisbe'.

78

Shakespeare myth no. 6

Shakespeare has the largest vocabulary of any English writer.

Far from it. Any modern writer uses far more words than Shakespeare. It's reckoned that by the end of the 16th century there were around 150,000 words in English. Shakespeare's plays contain about 20,000 different words (excluding variants of the same word, like plurals and different tenses). That's quite a fair percentage of those available to him. But English has swelled enormously since then. The unabridged *Oxford English Dictionary* now lists 600,000 words. We don't use them all to chat, but an averagely educated person today has about 50,000 words at their command. Even allowing for words that Shakespeare knew but didn't use in writing, that's more than twice his vocabulary.

It's not what you've got but how you use it!

POLONIUS: What do you read,
    my lord?

HAMLET: Words, words, words.

Hamlet, Act II scene 2

A hope lost

1596 proved a tragic year for Will. In August his son Hamnet died. He was 11 years old. Anne was now 40 and unlikely to have more children. Will was 32, no longer young by the standards of the time. To lose an only son, who would have carried on the family name and guaranteed support in his old age, was a bitter blow. It may seem that Will was not much of a family man and had had little contact with his son, but there's no reason to think he didn't spend as much time with his family as work allowed. Aubrey reports that he went home every year.

Life's but a walking shadow,
a poor player
That struts and frets his hour
upon the stage
And then is heard no more.

Macbeth, Act V scene 5

The plays in brief
King John
1595~1597

Shakespeare was working on *King John* about the time Hamnet died, and one passage perhaps gives us a clue to his feelings. The play's general tone of cynical political double-crossing is suddenly lit up by a lyrical outburst of grief as Lady Constance mourns her young son:

Grief fills the room up of my absent child,
Lies in his bed, walks up and down with me,
Puts on his pretty looks, repeats his words,
Remembers me of all his gracious parts,
Stuffs out his vacant garments with his form;
Then have I reason to be fond of grief?

Constance, mother to England's rightful heir, is the one steadfast light in the play's murky world. Will has his hands tied by history's poor verdict on King John. He can't make the play heroic, so he presents it as politics in action. Power is up for grabs and all the main characters get their hands dirty.

In the end, the usurper John is poisoned and France and England patch up a peace. Will comments wryly through the mouth of Philip the Bastard:

Mad world! mad kings! mad composition!

The Merchant of Venice
1596~1597

We don't know whether Will's audiences liked *King John*, because no records of performances survive, but it has not been popular since. That can't be said of another play of this time: *The Merchant of Venice*.

This counts as a comedy, but it's rather a disconcerting one by today's ways of thinking. The plot is a mixture of fairytale and sharp dealing, with racist distinctions between 'good' characters and 'bad'. Will blends two folk themes: the bride who can only be won by choosing rightly between three caskets, and the debt that can only be paid with human flesh.

The Venetian Bassanio travels to Belmont, chooses the right casket and wins his love Portia, but he has financed his trip by borrowing from his merchant friend, Antonio. Antonio's cash is tied up in goods at sea, but since his credit is good, Shylock, a Jewish moneylender, has lent him the sum. If it's not paid back on time, Shylock wants a pound of Antonio's flesh in exchange. Antonio has agreed light-heartedly because he assumes it'll never come to that – but his ship sinks, and it does!

Jews were stock hate figures in Christian folk tales. Christians made no allowance for the fact that moneylending was in Jewish hands because the Church had forbidden Christians to do it. Instead, they put it down to innate greed. Yet Will's instinctive feeling for the humanity of a character leads him in one direction, while the plot he's borrowed goes in another. Here is the 'bad' Jew's impassioned outburst against the 'good' Antonio's callous contempt for him:

Hath not a Jew eyes? Hath not a Jew hands, organs, dimensions, senses, affections, passions; fed with the same food . . . warmed and cooled by the same winter and summer as a Christian is? If you prick us, do we not bleed? If you tickle us, do we not laugh? If you poison us, do we not die? And if you wrong us, do we not revenge?

Though he ignores Portia's plea for mercy and is ready to carve Antonio's living flesh, it is impossible not to feel for the wrongs Shylock has suffered. Cheated by a technicality of his not unprovoked revenge, stripped of his wealth, forced to become Christian – his utter humiliation enables everyone else to be happy. In Will's hands a folk tale has strayed into real life, and shows the strain as a traditional ending is forced upon it.

Portia, disguised as a famous lawyer, tries to persuade Shylock to abandon his revenge.

More disappointed hope

There is another sad twist to the story of Hamnet's death. Many years earlier John Shakespeare had applied to the Garter King of Arms[1] for the grant of a coat of arms, but finding the application too expensive he had dropped it. Now Will was earning enough to help his father take it up again. In 1596, on Will's instigation, John Shakespeare was granted a coat of arms showing a silver-tipped spear (a pun on his name) and the bold motto *Non sanz droict* (Not without right). The sketch for it has a rather belittling scribble on it from a herald of the College of Arms: 'Shakespear ye player'.

The award raised John to the status of 'gentleman', a distinction his descendants would inherit. This was a matter of importance in the class-conscious Elizabethan world. Will was no revolutionary. His plays have many reflections on the wisdom of preserving the proper order of society, and there's no doubt that the grant gave him great

1. *the head of the College of Arms, which controls the use of coats of arms.*

satisfaction. It would give the lie to critics who sneered at him as a country upstart and, more importantly, his descendants would establish the name of Shakespeare as that of a distinguished family of Warwickshire gentlefolk. But by October, when the grant was finally processed, Hamnet was dead and such hopes were gone.

Oft expectation fails, and
most oft there
Where most it promises; and oft
it hits
Where hope is coldest, and despair
most fits.

All's Well that Ends Well, Act II scene 1

A house fit for a gentleman

There is no doubt that a lot of Will's heart was in Warwickshire. Throughout his working life in London he lived in rented lodgings. When he felt he could afford to buy a house he bought one in Stratford, not in the capital.

In 1597 he became the owner of New Place, one of Stratford's finest houses. It set the seal on his standing in his place of birth. Later he enlarged the garden by buying additional land and by demolishing a cottage. He used the barns to store corn and barley. It was a time of harvest failure and short supplies. The price of grain had quadrupled, and a few months after buying New Place Will was recorded disapprovingly as hoarding 8 bushels (= 64 gallons or 291 litres) of malt there. The writer of immortal poetry had inherited a business instinct from his father.

Estate agents as we know them didn't exist in Elizabethan England, but what might the blurb have been like if they had?

FOR SALE

NEW PLACE, STRATFORD

Universally agreed to be one of the finest properties in town, this imposing 15th-century brick and timber residence is centrally situated, standing most conveniently at the junction of Chapel Street and Chapel Lane. The attractive property comprises, amongst a host of other features, a messuage with 10 fireplaces, having bay windows to the east, a well, two barns with appurtenances, and a 180-foot (55-metre) garden with orchards, together with the opportunity to acquire more land.

In need of some restoration.

Henry IV Parts I and II
Henry V
1596, 1598, 1599

During this period Will returns to the theme of what makes a good monarch, taking up England's story from the point he reached at the close of *Richard II*.

Henry IV Part I opens with King Henry (formerly Bolingbroke) struggling to assert his authority over nobles who dispute his right to rule. Prominent among them is the reckless firebrand Harry Hotspur (otherwise Henry Percy, heir to the earldom of Northumberland). Another thorn in Henry's side is his own son Prince Hal, who is not shaping up well as heir to the throne.

From a hint Will found in Holinshed's *Chronicles*, suggesting the prince had too many idle friends, he creates a parallel world to the world of kingship and good governance which is the proper concern of princes – a tavern world of boasters, bawds and thieves, a world without honour or principle, where nothing is sacred but good fellowship and the pleasure of the moment. Hal joins in the worst of it, a prince of rogues, but always with the sense (that Will lets the audience share) that his true place is elsewhere.

The sequence of three plays develops the theme of the making of a good king. At the moment of crisis Hal shows himself strong and resolute. He sheds his low friends and steps into his father's shoes to become one of England's A-rated monarchs – the valiant Henry V who leads his men to glorious victory at Agincourt. But Will has booby-trapped his royal path (unintentionally, surely?) by making his low-life cronies so appealing that his rejection of them chills us in a way that's hard to forgive:

'How agrees the devil and thee about thy soul, that thou soldest him on Good Friday last for a cup of madeira and a cold capon's leg?' Hal asks his old friend Falstaff in the days of their comradeship.

'Go hang thyself in thine own heir-apparent garters' is Falstaff's comeback, sure of the good terms they're on.

It's a different picture when Falstaff hails the new king, Henry V, on his coronation:

I know thee not, old man: fall to thy prayers;
How ill white hairs become a fool and jester!
I have long dream'd of such a type of man,
So surfeit-swelled,[1] so old and so profane.[2]

1. *surfeit-swelled: swelled up by overindulgence.*
2. *profane: unholy.*

Will's greatest comic creation, the fat knight Falstaff, breaks every rule in the book. He is grossly oversized – 'a tub of lard' – old, vain, boastful, cowardly and with not a scrap of conscience. Yet he is the embodiment of good cheer, exuding the joys of being a great eater, drinker and out-and-out slacker.

He doesn't appear in person in *Henry V*, though his death (in bed) is touchingly reported. But that was not the end of him. He was such a favourite with audiences that Will had to write a 'vehicle' especially for him...

The plays in brief
The Merry Wives of Windsor
1597~1598

Legend says that Queen Elizabeth wanted a play showing Falstaff in love. The result was this good-natured comedy in which Falstaff propositions two well-behaved Windsor ladies in the hopes of getting at their husbands' money. They completely outsmart him, at one point getting him into a laundry basket and dropping him in the Thames. Great fun, but not the Bard's masterpiece.

Some Shakespearean insults

Both parts of *Henry IV* are replete with juicy put-downs. Here are just a few:

Henry IV Part I

You starveling, you eel-skin, you dried neat's tongue, you bull's pizzle, you stockfish – O for breath to utter what is like thee! – you tailor's yard, you sheath, you bow-case, you vile standing tuck!

Thou clay-brained guts, thou knotty-pated fool, Thou whoreson obscene tallow-catch!

Henry IV Part II

Away, you bottle-rascal, you basket-hilt stale juggler you.

Thou damn'd tripe-visaged rascal.

You scullion! You rampallion! You fustilarian! I'll tickle your catastrophe!

The first Globe

All the world's a stage, and all the men and women merely players.

As You Like It, *Act II scene 7*

CHAPTER FIVE

AT THE GLOBE

n 1598 the Chamberlain's Men were in crisis – literally shut out of their own theatre. James Burbage had built it; the very idea of a theatre was his brainchild. How could any one else have a claim to it?

But James had built the Theatre on rented land. After 21 years the lease was up and the landlord would not renew it. He objected to the Burbages as unruly tenants. Cuthbert and Richard Burbage, who had taken over the building after their father's death, thought of a neat way to outwit him. He could keep the land, but they would have the theatre! They rented another plot of ground on Bankside, south of the river, and, on a snowy day just after Christmas 1598, when most people were snug indoors, they got a builder to surreptitiously pull the old theatre down and transport its valuable long timbers over the river. The landlord was furious and tried for three years to sue them, but to no effect.

The forced migration proved a good move for the company. Bankside was traditionally the place where Londoners went to enjoy themselves (even a Roman gladiator's trident has been dug up there). It was outside the city boundary, so anything went: alehouses and brothels, bear-baiting, cockfighting, bullrings, bowling alleys that doubled as gambling dens – and, of course, theatres. The Swan and the Rose were already well established.

This became Will's new workplace. There's every reason to think he relished its humming life. He took lodgings in the surrounding neighbourhood of Southwark. There were plenty of places to choose from, some less disorderly than others.

At the Globe

The Globe was in a rowdy part of London, and audiences could not be relied on to listen in respectful silence. Actors and playwrights had their work cut out to hold the attention of the 'groundlings' who stood in the unroofed pit.

Galleries

Atlas (column in the shape of a male figure)

Column supporting stage roof

Barrier at front of stage

Groundlings

Packed tightly into the available space, the spectators must often have been jostled and distracted, especially when vendors elbowed their way through the crowd to sell beer and snacks.

Fruit seller

Critic

Cutpurse (thief)

...with diverse and many
unlawful and offensive weapons...
breaking and throwing down the
said Theatre in very outrageous,
violent and riotous sort.

Eyewitness Gyles Allen

The Chamberlain's Men named their new theatre the Globe, a bold title that boasted it presented the whole world on its stage. Since its frame was built with the Theatre's old timbers it must have been around the same size, but it was altogether grander and more lavishly decorated. People paid a penny (half the price of a pint of good ale) to enter. If you wanted a seat you paid another penny at the stairs leading to the galleries. A seat with a cushion cost a third penny. The stage was at the groundlings' eye level, so everyone had a clear view of the players. The galleries were roofed and the stage was sheltered by an overhanging roof of its own, but if it rained the audience in the yard got drenched.

Players came on through two entrances at the back of the stage. There was no curtain, no lighting (none was needed – performances were always in the afternoon) and no scenery apart from the occasional prop – such as a throne or a general's tent – that was carried on to suggest a setting.

Spectacular effects were conjured up by magnificent costumes, splendid processions and vigorous battle scenes, and by the magic of words. As soon as the last of three trumpet blasts warned that the play was starting, the opening players strode onto the stage. They had to capture the audience's attention at once, without the help of a rising curtain and dimmed lights. The action was kept going fast, with no scene breaks or interval. People listened intently. A spectator looking down from the galleries recalled seeing the heads of the groundlings swaying in unison as emotion ran through them.

Even using the old timbers, the Globe cost a lot to build. Money was raised by selling shares in it. The Burbage brothers held half the shares. The other half was split between five senior company members, one of whom was Will Shakespeare. It was a shrewd move for him. He now owned a tenth of this splendid new theatre, and a tenth of its profits would be his.

Apparel

Good play-scripts were valuable assets, but a company invested far more money in what was termed 'apparel' (costumes and props). Up close, in the glare of daylight, stage nobility had to look just like the real thing. Often they wore the nearly-new cast-offs of real-life nobles.

Costumes specially made could almost literally cost a fortune. A black velvet cloak 'with sleeves embrodered [sic] all with silver and gold' cost £20. 10s. 6d. – more than a third of the sum Shakespeare paid for New Place. No wonder the heaviest fine a player could incur was for leaving the playhouse still wearing the company's apparel.

> For the apparel oft proclaims the man.[1]

1. Hamlet, *Act I scene 3.*

An afternoon at the Globe

One of the plays that opened the Globe's first season was Will's *Julius Caesar*. Luckily for us, a Swiss tourist called Thomas Platter went to a performance of it on 21 September 1599 and described it in his diary:

> *Saw the tragedy of the first emperor Julius Caesar, very pleasingly performed, with about 15 characters; at the end of the play they danced together admirably and gracefully, according to their custom, two in each group dressed in men's and two in women's apparel.*

That might seem a strange ending for this severe play, but some form of comical afterpiece with singing and dancing, known as the 'jig', was performed after every play, to send the groundlings home in a cheery mood.

The plays in brief
Julius Caesar
1599

Julius Caesar explores one of life's great dilemmas: does the end justify the means? Republican Rome is celebrating the return of Caesar, its great military leader, after a splendid victory. The common people are jubilant, but more thoughtful citizens suspect that Caesar has plans to get himself made king. A group of them plot to assassinate him, from the best of motives – to preserve the traditional freedoms of the Roman Republic.

The assassination succeeds, but the conspirators cannot control its aftermath. Their leaders, Cassius and Brutus, have diverging agendas. Cassius, irascible but far-sighted, sees the need to shed more blood. The totally honourable Brutus will not let him. And so the crucial mistake is made: the charismatic Mark Antony, great friend of Caesar, is not only spared but allowed to speak at Caesar's funeral.

Brutus speaks first, telling the assembled crowd, in all sincerity, that the conspirators acted solely for the people's good. The people listen and agree. But Will has a dramatist's trick up his sleeve. He makes Brutus give his well-reasoned arguments in prose. Then Mark Antony takes centre stage and, in a famous scene, addresses the crowd in the highly charged language of verse, manipulating his listeners with all the arts of oratory until they are baying for the blood of people whom, only moments ago, they were applauding.

From this point the play is the tragedy of Brutus rather than of Caesar. Driven to doubt the integrity of his once-dear friend, Cassius, Brutus quarrels with him against his will. Their forces are defeated in battle by Mark Antony's coalition and both Cassius and Brutus die the noble death of running on their own swords.

Were Brutus's actions morally justified? Will does not take sides. But these are the words of the conspirators' enemy, Antony, spoken over Brutus's body:

This was the noblest Roman of them all;
All the conspirators, save only he,
Did that they did in envy of great Caesar;
He only, in a general honest thought
And common good to all, made one of them.
His life was gentle; and the elements
So mix'd in him, that Nature might stand up
And say to all the world, 'This was a man!'

Why do Shakespeare's characters talk in verse?

Nearly all plays in Shakespeare's day were written in verse. The lofty language of poetry was thought appropriate for serious drama about high-born characters. Prose was used in comic exchanges or for the speech of servants and ordinary people.

Blank verse, the metre used by Elizabethan dramatists, is not very far removed from normal English speech. It's hard to speak English without some sort of rhythm because it is a 'stress-timed' language – meaning that it is formed of stressed and unstressed syllables, with the stressed ones coming at fairly regular intervals – a sort of 'te-tum, te-tum, te-tum'. Blank verse (called 'blank' because it does not rhyme) takes this rhythm and regularises it into lines of five stresses or beats: *te-tum te-tum te-tum te-tum te-tum*.

The art of the poet lies in making variations on this underlying pattern, by juggling with the stresses. Shakespeare was supreme at this, especially in the later plays. He reverses the beat – 'tum-te' – or has successive beats of a single strongly stressed syllable, so that the expected rhythm and the unexpected play against each other; he adds extra unstressed syllables; he breaks the line between two speakers. He uses all these variants within four

lines to capture Hamlet's fevered state of mind
as he confronts his mother:

HAMLET: Nay, but to live
 In the rank sweat of an enseamed bed,
 Stewed in corruption, honeying and making
          love
 Over the nasty sty –
GERTRUDE: O, speak to me no more!

Hamlet, Act III scene 4

Will was now at the midpoint of his career,
writing in top gear. And, remember, he was
acting too – perhaps not full-time now that he
was a sharer, but he is listed as a player in rival
playwright Ben Jonson's *Sejanus* in 1603, so
he was having to learn parts written by other
people as well! (According to Jonson, this
performance of *Sejanus* was a flop.)

During and just after the move to the Globe,
Will came up with three comedy greats : *Much
Ado about Nothing*, *As You like It* and *Twelfth
Night*. Each has its own particular flavour but
they are alike in each having one of Will's
most appealing heroines.

Much Ado about Nothing
1598~1599

This play is based on an Italian tale about a pair of lovers (Will names them Hero and Claudio), whose happiness is very nearly ruined by a villainous deception.

But Will throws in another couple of his own invention who are so lively that they take over the play. Benedick declares he's a confirmed bachelor; feisty, quick-witted Beatrice tells everyone she cannot stand him. Whenever they meet there are verbal fireworks:

BEATRICE: *I wonder that you will still[1] be talking, Signor Benedick. Nobody marks[2] you.*
BENEDICK: *What, my dear Lady Disdain! Are you yet living?*
BEATRICE: *Is it possible that disdain should die while she hath such meet[3] food to feed it as Signor Benedick? Courtesy itself must convert to disdain if you come in her presence.*
BENEDICK: *Then is courtesy a turncoat. But it is certain I am loved of all ladies, only you excepted. And I would[4] I could find it in my heart that I had not a hard heart, for truly I love none.*
BEATRICE: *A dear happiness to women.*

1. *still: always.*   2. *marks: pays attention to.*   3. *meet: suitable.*
4. *I would: I wish.*

Not a promising start for a romance! But the long-standing 'merry war' between them prompts their friends to make fools of them by getting them to fall in love with each other. Through eavesdropping on conversations set up to be overheard, each is made to believe the other is secretly pining for them. That does the trick! Beatrice proves as swift in falling in love as in verbal attack:

And, Benedick, love on. I will requite thee,[1]
Taming my wild heart to thy loving hand.

Each abandons their old mock-hostility through a generous impulse to spare the other's feelings, and, after a certain amount of anguish required by the Hero and Claudio story, the play ends, as comedy must, in happy weddings – a pair of them.

Speak low if you speak love.

Act II scene 1

I love you with so much of my heart that none is left to protest.

Act IV scene 1

1. *requite thee: love you in return.*

The plays in brief
As You Like It
1599~1600

Unlike Beatrice – unaware that her constant mockery of Benedick shows she's obsessed with him – Rosalind in *As You like It* knows only too well she's in love with dispossessed young noble, Orlando.

'O coz, coz, coz, my pretty little coz,' she bursts out to her cousin Celia, 'That thou didst know how many fathoms deep I am in love! But it cannot be sounded: my affection hath an unknown bottom, like the bay of Portugal.'

Unfortunately she must hide it. The plot requires her not to shed the boy's disguise she has put on in fleeing her vengeful uncle and seeking refuge in the Forest of Arden. Happily, Orlando, also a forest refugee, has been fly-posting the trees with love poems in her praise, not realising that Rosalind and Ganymede, the spirited young man he meets in the forest, are one and the same. Will contrives a deliciously involved wooing between them, with Rosalind as the prime mover. She offers to cure lovesick Orlando through role-play therapy. She will act the part of Rosalind and be so capriciously feminine he'll soon be rid of love. The audience can feel the giddy happiness this stratagem allows her as she drinks love in while pretending to reject it:

ROSALIND: Am I not your Rosalind?

ORLANDO: I take some joy to say you are, because I would be talking of her.

ROSALIND: Well, in her person I say, I will not have you.

ORLANDO: Then, in mine own person I die.

ROSALIND: No, faith, die by attorney.[1] The poor world is almost six thousand years old and in all this time there was not one man died in his own person, videlicet,[2] for love ... Men have died from time to time and worms have eaten them, but not for love.

ORLANDO: I would not have my right Rosalind of this mind for, I protest, her frown might kill me.

ROSALIND: By this hand it will not kill a fly. But come now, I will be your Rosalind in a more coming-on mood; ask me what you will, I will grant it.

ORLANDO: Then love me, Rosalind.

ROSALIND: Yes, faith, will I, Fridays and Saturdays and all.

Of course, all ends well. The world of *As You Like It* is dappled woodland sunshine untouched by real sorrow, and its frank and joyous heroine is one of the most appealing that Will created.

1. *by attorney:* by proxy; that is, get someone else to die on your behalf.
2. *videlicet:* namely, specifically.

The plays in brief
Twelfth Night
1601~1602

With suitable dress and wigs, an all-male cast can make the boy/girl conundrum amazingly convincing on stage. Will uses it again in *Twelfth Night*, with the added complication that the disguised heroine has a twin brother (supposed dead) whose return (of which she's unaware) creates even more identity confusion.

The play opens with the extravagantly lovesick Duke of Illyria pining for Olivia, a lady who has sworn to see no man during a seven years' mourning for her brother. Meanwhile, the twins Viola and Sebastian have been parted in a shipwreck off the Illyrian coast. Viola fears her brother is drowned, and sorrowfully prepares to face the world alone.

Next we are in Olivia's household where the maid, Maria, is scolding Olivia's imperturbably drunken uncle, Sir Toby Belch, for disturbing the house with his racketing and for sponging off a rich nincompoop, Sir Andrew Aguecheek, by persuading him to woo Olivia. Will sets three worlds in play: the world of true feeling, of which Viola is the grave and thoughtful centre; the fancied emotion of the Duke's posturing and Olivia's self-cloistering; and the riotous world of Sir Toby's gang.

The worlds soon collide. Viola disguises herself as a boy, calling herself Cesario, and gets employment as servant to the Duke. He takes such a liking to Cesario that he uses 'him' as a go-between in his wooing of Olivia. This is agony for Viola, who has fallen in love with the Duke but must now declare how much he loves someone else.

Viola's own feeling finds expression in voicing another's:

VIOLA: If I did love you in my master's flame,
*   With such a suffering, such a deadly life,*
*   In your denial I would find no sense;*
*   I would not understand it.*
OLIVIA: Why, what would you?
VIOLA: Make me a willow cabin at your gate
*   And call upon the soul within the house;*
*   Write loyal cantons¹ of contemned² love,*
*   And sing them loud even in the dead of night;*
*   Holla your name to the reverberate hills,*
*   And make the babbling gossip of the air*
*   Cry out 'Olivia!' O, you should not rest*
*   Between the elements of earth and air*
*   But you should pity me!*

This pleading has an effect, but not the one intended: Olivia is smitten by the handsome Cesario. The Duke makes Viola's misery worse by idly inquiring into Cesario's love-life while trumpeting his own superior passion:

---

1. *cantons: verses, stanzas.*
2. *contemned: scorned, held in contempt.*

DUKE: Make no compare
  Between the love a woman can bear me
  And that I owe Olivia.
VIOLA: Ay, but I know –
DUKE: What dost thou know?
VIOLA: Too well what love women to men may
          owe:
  In faith, they have as true a heart as we.
  My father had a daughter lov'd a man,
  As it might be, perhaps, were I a woman,
  I should your lordship.
DUKE: And what's her history?
VIOLA: A blank, my lord. She never told her
          love,
  But let concealment, like a worm i' the bud,
  Feed on her damask[1] cheek: she pin'd in
          thought
  And, with a green and yellow melancholy,
  She sat like Patience on a monument,
  Smiling at grief.

Meanwhile, the 'below-stairs' characters are
bent on mischief. Olivia's tight-lipped,
puritanical steward Malvolio has got on the
wrong side of them by trying, ineffectually, to
curb Sir Toby.

SIR TOBY: Dost thou think, because thou art
  virtuous, there shall be no more cakes and
  ale? . . . Go, sir, rub your chain[2] with crumbs.

1. damask: rose-cloured.
2. rub your chain: polish your chain of office (he is insulting Malvolio
by reminding him that he is a servant).

Toby, Maria, Sir Andrew and Feste the clown plan revenge. Their plot hinges on Malvolio's known vanity and ambition. They let him find a forged letter, apparently from Olivia, in which she declares a secret passion for him. Fantasising about the power he'll wield as Olivia's husband, he follows the letter's hints to appear before her in cross-gartered yellow stockings and to be constantly smiling (a fashion and manner that Maria knows her mistress hates).

The plot works admirably. Olivia is convinced Malvolio is insane, and tells Sir Toby to take care of him: 'I would not have him miscarry[1] for half my dowry.'[2] The conspirators tie him up in a dark room and subject him to mocking interrogations designed to show how mad he is. Their fun is cruel, and Will's instinctive feeling for the underdog gives Malvolio dignity in his humiliation:

> Good fool, help me to some light and paper. I tell thee I am as well in my wits as any man in Illyria.

1. *miscarry*: come to harm.
2. *dowry*: a gift of money or property made by a bride's family to her husband; without it, a woman has no chance of making an advantageous marriage.

Meanwhile Sir Andrew has worked himself into a froth of jealousy over Olivia's fondness for Cesario (really Viola, remember). Encouraged by Sir Toby, he challenges Cesario to a duel. But Sebastian is now safe ashore, and when Sir Andrew draws his sword on the youth he thinks is Cesario he gets much more than he bargained for. Sir Toby joins the fray, and he and Sebastian are only prevented from carving each other up by the entry of Olivia. She halts the fight to save the supposed Cesario, greeting Sebastian with sweet words, and finally proposing marriage. Completely bewildered, he is delighted to accept.

Everything unravels in the last act, but only after the Duke has spurned Viola in fury on hearing Olivia declare that she and Cesario are married. The arrival of Sir Andrew and Sir Toby with their heads all bloodied, and of Sebastian apologising for having sliced them, throws everyone into amazement:

DUKE: *One face, one voice, one habit[1] and two persons!*

ANTONIO: *An apple cleft in two is not more twin Than these two creatures.*

Viola is doubly rewarded for her suffering and faithful love: by reunion with her beloved brother, and by the Duke's dawning realisation

1. *habit: costume.*

112

that a treasure truly worth loving was there by his side all along.

The only deeply injured heart is Malvolio's. Olivia will see him reinstated in his job, but that is no balm to his pride. His exit line 'I'll be revenged on the whole pack of you!' is a cry of impotent rage.

The interweaving of comical deceptions, misperceptions and true suffering gives *Twelfth Night* an unmistakable tinge of melancholy in the midst of its laughter, which makes many people rate it the most rounded and subtlest of the comedies.

If music be the food of love,
play on,
Give me excess of it; that,
surfeiting,[1]
The appetite may sicken,
and so die.

Act I scene 1

1. *surfeiting: eating too much.*

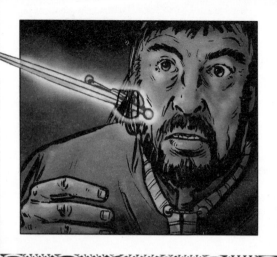

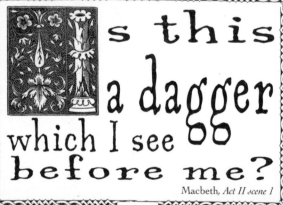

s this a dagger which I see before me?

Macbeth, *Act II scene 1*

CHAPTER SIX

THE GREAT TRAGEDIES

 t the same time that he was writing in this rich comedy vein, Will was also at work on the first of what we now think of as his four great tragedies: *Hamlet*, *King Lear*, *Macbeth* and *Othello*.

Tragedy and comedy

When Shakespeare's friends Heminges and Condell collected his works together for publication (see page 169) they divided his plays into comedies, histories and tragedies. That might seem clear enough to us – comedies make you laugh, histories re-enact events, and tragedies show sufferings without a happy outcome – but Shakespeare and his contemporaries saw the terms slightly differently.

Essentially, tragedy was poetic and lofty; it showed people of high rank falling from greatness. Thus Shakespeare's *Richard II* was originally classed as a tragedy, not a history. Comedy could contain both high and low characters. It could provoke laughter, but also come close to tears, provided it had a happy ending. Shakespeare's late comedies are sometimes called 'romantic'. This is a 19th-century term (nothing to do with modern love stories) coined to describe their special blend of fairytale otherworldliness with themes of reconciliation and forgiveness. No belly-laughs there!

Hamlet
c. 1600

Even if you can't recite a single speech from Shakespeare, you know one line for sure. No need to quote it here, but it's the quintessence of the self-doubt that consumes Hamlet on being instructed, by the ghost of his murdered father, to act the avenger and kill his usurping uncle. It's a role that he's obviously not cut out for:

The time is out of joint – O cursed spite,
That ever I was born to set it right!

Hamlet puts off action because he is unsure of himself and unsure of the truth. Nothing is as it seems; nothing can be trusted. He even doubts his love, the innocent Ophelia, and taunts her savagely. He feigns madness in order to investigate his father's death – or is he really mad? The audience must make up its mind on that. He is swift enough in action in the second half of the play, dealing ruthlessly with the spies his uncle has set upon him and returning to wreak a vengeance that leaves the stage well strewn with bodies.

At this level Hamlet is a thrilling revenge drama, spiced with intrigue, murder and madness. With Richard Burbage in the title role it was an immediate success, and it has never been off the stage since. At another level it is all about thought. Hamlet (as is well known) is moody and into questioning things: Is revenge just? Is life worth living? Are we any better than the brute beasts?

O, that this too too solid flesh would melt,
Thaw and resolve itself into a dew!

Act I scene 2

To die, to sleep;
To sleep: perchance to dream: ay, there's the rub:
For in that sleep of death what dreams may come,
When we have shuffled off this mortal coil,
Must give us pause:

Act III scene 1

Soliloquy

Drama is story told through action, so how can *thought* be staged? Will does it by making inspired use of soliloquy (meaning 'talking to oneself')[1] – a common device on the Elizabethan stage for putting an audience quickly in the picture. A character speaks as if to no-one (but really to the audience), to reveal what sort of person he is and what he means to do:

> *... since I cannot prove a lover*
> *To entertain these fair, well-spoken days,*
> *I am determined to prove a villain,*
> *And hate the idle pleasures of these days.*

declares the duke of Gloucester, shaping up to become wicked King Richard III.

By the time he was writing *Hamlet* Will had developed the soliloquy into an infinitely more subtle tool. Hamlet's troubled meditations can run to nearly 60 lines non-stop without seeming forced or non-dramatic. They are the drama of a mind in action:

> *Who would fardels[2] bear,*
> *To grunt and sweat under a weary life,*
> *But that the dread of something after death,*
> *The undiscover'd country from whose bourn[3]*
> *No traveller returns, puzzles the will,*
> *And makes us rather bear the ills we have,*
> *Than fly to others that we know not of?*

1. from Latin solus *'alone'* and loqui *'to speak'*.
2. fardels: burdens.
3. bourn: boundary.

Shakespeare, director

Can Hamlet's father's ghost be trusted, or is it a demon from hell? To settle this tormenting question Hamlet asks some players to act a story mirroring the ghost's, so that if King Claudius is guilty he will betray it. Hamlet has plenty to say on the way he wants it acted, and it's hard to believe that Will hadn't given much the same advice to players who mangled his lines. In his day there were no directors – the actors worked things out together – but this, surely, is Will doing what we would call directing:

Speak the speech . . . as I pronounced it to you, trippingly on the tongue: but if you mouth it, as many of your players do, I had as lief[1] the town crier spoke my lines. Nor do not saw the air too much with your hands, thus, but use it gently: for in the very torrent, tempest and whirlwind of passion, you must beget . . . a temperance that may give it smoothness. . . . Suit the action to the word, the word to the action; . . . that you o'erstep not the modesty of nature: for anything so overdone is from the purpose of playing, whose end . . . is to hold, as 'twere, the mirror up to nature.

---

1. *I had as lief: I would rather.*

The plays in brief
Othello
c.1603~1604

Hamlet is a play of perplexities and hesitations. In contrast, the tragedy of *Othello* lies in the speed with which emotions are translated into action. In its essence the plot is simple, a drama of domestic violence: a good man is misled, through the evil actions of a supposed friend, into believing that his adored young bride is faithless. In an uncontrollable passion of jealousy he murders her, only to learn almost immediately that she was innocent.

Will took the bare bones of the plot from an Italian story in which the hero is a highly esteemed Venetian 'Moor' – a black man. And black he remains in the play. Characters with an interest in bad-mouthing Othello – Brabanzio, furious that his daughter Desdemona has married against his will, and, above all, Othello's ensign Iago, the embodiment of vengefulness – use racist insults as the weapon to hand. In all other ways Othello's race is not an issue. What matters is the unfolding calamity of a noble heart destroyed by its inability to conceive of treachery in those it trusts.

Will lets the audience see what Othello doesn't: the motiveless evil of Iago, who is controlling events. In his trumped-up evidence against

Desdemona Iago relies on the passionate directness of Othello, who is compelled by the deepest love to suffer the most frenzied jealousy and to vent it in immediate action.

Othello learns his wife's innocence while he is still cradling her lifeless body in his arms. On the point of taking his own life, he asks to be judged only according to the truth:

>   *... nothing extenuate,*
> *Nor set down aught in malice: then you must speak*
> *Of one that loved not wisely but too well;*
> *Of one not easily jealous, but, being wrought,*
> *Perplex'd in the extreme; of one whose hand,*
> *Like the base Indian, threw a pearl away*
> *Richer than all his tribe.*

The Moor is of a free and open nature,

That thinks men honest that but seem to be so.

Act I scene 3

122

The plays in brief
King Lear
1605~1606

Thought by many to be his greatest achievement, Will's next tragedy is a shattering experience – not obviously an entertainment to put bums on seats (or yobs in the yard?). Yet Will wrote parts he knew the company's players could tackle and plays he knew its audience could appreciate – which says a lot for the serious attention that a holiday crowd of ordinary Londoners was prepared to give a play, in his day.

Lear begins as a folk tale: a foolish old king gives his kingdom away to his three daughters, dividing it according to the amount that each daughter says she loves him. Taking their answers at face value, he gives everything to his deceitful elder daughters and nothing to the tongue-tied youngest.

In character the king is the opposite of Hamlet. He has no self-knowledge. He thinks that kingship is in the very nature of his being. The agony of the play lies in his discovery that, in its essence, a human being is nothing. Experience is Lear's teacher. Stripped by his elder daughters of everything – authority, possessions, followers, even shelter – he is driven out into a night of terrible storm, to survive however he may, amongst beggars and madmen. As his brain fragments into madness his understanding is alight:

> Poor naked wretches, wheresoe'er you are,
> That bide[1] the pelting of this pitiless storm,
> How shall your houseless heads and unfed
>   sides,
> Your loop'd and window'd[2] raggedness, defend
>   you
> From seasons such as these? O, I have ta'en
> Too little care of this! Take physic,[3] pomp;
> Expose thyself to feel what wretches feel,
> That thou mayst shake the superflux[4] to them
> And show the heavens more just.

Restored to his truly-loving daughter, Cordelia, the crazed Lear has reached a point where even loss of liberty is a happiness to him, if she is at his side:

>   . . . Come, let's away to prison.
> We two alone will sing like birds i' the cage:
> When thou dost ask me blessing, I'll kneel
>   down
> And ask of thee forgiveness: so we'll live,
> And pray, and sing, and tell old tales . . .

1. bide: endure.
2. loop'd and window'd: full of holes.
3. physic: medicine.
4. superflux: excess, leftovers.

What a touching end for a tragedy – madness assuaged by love. But Will is having none of that! Cordelia is murdered; Lear dies of heartbreak. So, what meaning did their sufferings have? *King Lear* is the extreme example of a perplexity that Will grapples with in several plays: does life have any meaning – unless meaning lies in the spirit with which we face life?

Blow, winds, and crack your cheeks! Rage, blow!
You cataracts and hurricanoes, spout
Till you have drench'd our steeples, drown'd the cocks![1]
You sulphurous and thought-executing fires,
Vaunt-couriers[2] to oak-cleaving thunderbolts,
singe my white head!

Act III scene 2

1. *cocks: weathercocks.*
2. *Vaunt-couriers: scouts who go ahead of an army to clear the way.*

Richard Burbage

The role of Lear was created by Burbage. He was the company's top star, acclaimed as the greatest actor of his day. Only Edward Alleyn of the Admiral's Men could compare with him. He created all Shakespeare's great tragic heroes: *Hamlet, Lear, Macbeth, Othello*. The stereotype of Hamlet stripped to his shirt in his (assumed?) madness goes back to Burbage, as described by the poet Anthony Scoloker in 1604.

His performances were a huge element in the success of the Chamberlain's Men. He was a friend as well as a working colleague of Shakespeare, who left him 26 shillings in his will to buy a ring in memory of him. Evidently Burbage was hot-tempered: there is an account of him chasing off a creditor with a broom handle. He was an amateur painter too. It's even been suggested he did the portrait from which that po-faced engraving that fronts so many 'Complete Works' was taken.

He died in 1619, acting to the end – he never retired. His death was commemorated in a neat epitaph: 'Exit Burbage.'

from Tudor to Stuart

In 1606 Will seems to have done a bit of clever product placement. England now had a new monarch and the players, like everyone else, hoped to do well by seeking his favour.

The old Queen had died in 1603 after a reign of 45 years. She had no direct descendants, so with her the Tudor dynasty came to an end. For many years she had been pressed to name her heir, but this she would never do, believing, quite rightly, that anyone with an acknowledged right to rule was a threat to the sitting monarch. Her cousin, Mary Queen of Scots, had been executed for posing just this threat. (Catholics had regarded her as the true queen, since they considered Elizabeth's birth illegitimate.)

Ironically, when Elizabeth died it was Mary's son, James, who had the indisputable right to the English throne. Fortunately, he had been brought up a Protestant, so England was ready to welcome him. He made a triumphal entry into London as James VI of Scotland and James I of England.

James was a scholarly and cultivated man. He wrote poetry and was keenly interested in the theatre. A play that showed Banquo, ancestor of the Scottish kings, in a favourable light, that showed the wickedness of killing a rightful king, and furthermore involved witchcraft – a subject which James took very seriously – was sure to please him. So Will selected the story of the medieval usurper Macbeth for his next tragedy.

King James I and VI

The plays in brief
Macbeth
c.1606

Macbeth is the story of a lust for power that destroys a man. More darkly sinister than *Lear* or *Hamlet* (much of it takes place by night or in some murky spot), it presents evil as an active force.

The play opens with a scene of witchcraft. In the 1600s few people doubted the power of witches;[1] the three weird sisters ('weird' here having its old meaning of 'destiny-spinning') that Macbeth and Banquo meet on the wild heath would have seemed as terrible to the audience as they do to the two Scottish lords. Their prophecy, that Macbeth is destined to be king, enters like poison into his blood. He sees how it can be achieved, and the prospect horrifies him:

> Why do I yield to that suggestion
> Whose horrid image doth unfix my hair,[2]
> And make my seated heart knock at my ribs,
> Against the use of nature? Present fears
> Are less than horrible imaginings:
> My thought, whose murder yet is but
>   fantastical,[3]

1. King James I had even written a book on witchcraft, Daemonologie *(1597).*
2. unfix my hair: *make my hair stand on end.*
3. fantastical: *imaginary.*

Shakes so my single state of man that
function
Is smothered in surmise, and nothing is
But what is not.

It is his wife, Lady Macbeth, his 'dearest partner in greatness', who insists he must have the courage to do what is necessary – murder King Duncan, who will be sleeping that night in their house as an honoured guest.

'Give me the daggers,' she hisses at her husband as he staggers from the murder scene with them still in his hands; 'If he do bleed,/I'll gild the faces of the grooms withal,/That it may seem their gilt' (a hideous pun on 'gilt' and 'guilt').

Yet Lady Macbeth, so ruthless in her conscious mind, is destroyed by her unconscious self (where did Will get such insight into the modern theory of the unconscious?) which compels her to nightly sleepwalkings, in which she continually washes her hands of imagined blood yet cannot get them clean:

Yet here's a spot.... Out, damned spot! Out, I say!... Yet who would have thought the old man to have had so much blood in him?

With each bloody step he takes, Macbeth wishes he could turn back. 'Wake Duncan with thy knocking! I would thou couldst!' he shouts when he hears knocking on the door after the king's murder. But one step always entails another. Macbeth, now king, is not sure of his throne while Banquo lives. The weird sisters have foretold that Banquo's line will inherit it.[1]

'Fail not our feast,' Macbeth says to Banquo, warmly inviting him to a supper that he knows Banquo will not live to eat. But Banquo keeps the appointment – or Macbeth's distraught brain thinks he does. In a stunningly dramatic banqueting scene Macbeth recoils hysterically from the bloody ghost of his victim, while his wife and courtiers see nothing.

Macbeth and the ghost of Banquo

1. *James I believed that he was descended from Banquo.*

Drawn deeper and deeper into blood, as growing suspicion of him spurs him to more slaughter, Macbeth reaches a state where ambition is meaningless and all feeling deadened:

Tomorrow, and tomorrow, and tomorrow,
Creeps in this petty pace from day to day,
To the last syllable of recorded time;
And all our yesterdays have lighted fools
The way to dusty death. Out, out, brief candle!
Life's but a walking shadow; a poor player
That struts and frets his hour upon the stage
And then is heard no more: it is a tale
Told by an idiot, full of sound and fury,
Signifying nothing.

Realising he has been undone by the witches, whose promise that he is invincible proves to be doubletalk, Macbeth is left without hope; he cannot continue. 'I'll not fight with thee,' he tells Macduff who challenges him on the battlefield, but somehow, in his last moments, he finds the courage of total despair. 'Damned be him that first cries "Hold, enough!"' he cries, as they leave the stage, fighting to the death. And damned he knows he will be.

The Scottish play

That's how actors refer to *Macbeth*. It's thought to be so unlucky in the theatre that just saying its name spells disaster. The curse is said to go back to 1606 when the boy acting Lady Macbeth fell sick of a fever and died at the first performance. The tale is credited to the 17th-century diarist John Aubrey, though it's not mentioned in his writings.

Much better documented is the New York riot of 1849, when a feud between English actor William Charles Macready and American Edwin Forrest provoked a mob of Forrest's supporters to storm the Astor Theatre, where Macready was appearing as Macbeth. A crowd (said to number 20,000!) hurled brickbats and paving stones; the National Guard was called out and more than 20 people were killed.

Back in England, the Oldham Coliseum had a classic case of *Macbeth*-blight in 1947, when Macduff accidentally stabbed Macbeth for real. The wound became infected and the unlucky actor, Harold Norman, died a few days later. His ghost is said to appear regularly at the theatre, usually on Thursdays, the day he was stabbed.

133

Antony and Cleopatra
1606~1607

What a change to breathe the atmosphere of
Antony and Cleopatra – warm and dazzling, and
magnificent in its scope. It continues Rome's
political drama from the point where *Julius
Caesar* left off, but, unlike that quite sexless
play, the politics frames a passionate love story
– not the young, innocent love of *Romeo and
Juliet*, but mature, experienced and totally
besotted. Will brings all his poetic cunning
to the portrayal of the Queen of Egypt's
incomparable allure:

> *Age cannot wither her, nor custom stale
> Her infinite variety; other women cloy
> The appetites they feed, but she makes hungry
> Where most she satisfies.*

Cleopatra is a lustful 'gipsy' [*sic*] or a 'lass
unparalleled', depending on the speaker's
viewpoint. For her sake the great Roman
general Mark Antony neglects a soldier's
duties in order to feast and drink and love in
her arms. He recklessly antagonises Rome's new
leader, Octavius Caesar, who brings a force to
Egypt against him.

Antony is by now so enslaved by love that he has
lost the skill to command. He disregards the
advice of seasoned colleagues and loses to

Octavius at sea and on land. The lovers prefer
death to submitting to Rome. Antony dies in
Cleopatra's arms, inspiring in her this desolate
lament:

Hast thou no care of me? shall I abide
In this dull world, which in thy absence is
No better than a sty? O! see, my women,
The crown o' the earth doth melt. My lord!
O! wither'd is the garland of the war,
The soldier's pole[1] is fall'n; young boys
       and girls
Are level now with men; the odds[2] is gone,
And there is nothing left remarkable
Beneath the visiting moon.

Now boast thee, death, in thy
possession lies
A lass unparalleled.

Act V scene 2

1. *The soldier's pole: either the regimental standard, or the leader that*
soldiers looked to for guidance (as sailors looked to the Pole Star).
2. *the odds: that which was exceptional.*

Claudio condemned to death by Angelo

**e absolute
for death;
either
death or life**
Shall thereby be the sweeter.

Measure for Measure, *Act III scene 1*

THE PROBLEM PLAYS

ven at the peak of his London career, Will kept his eye on Stratford. His father died in 1601, which must have been the occasion for a sad visit. In May 1602 Will bought over 100 acres of farmland, costing £320, from Stratford friends. Later in the year he bought a small cottage in Chapel Lane, across from his own home, New Place. He was investing in his roots.

In 1605 he made what was, as far as we know, his largest single investment: £440 for the right to receive tithes (taxes) that were paid annually on land on the Welcombe Hills. They returned £60 a year. That's interest of around 14% – not a bad rate of return.

A brush with treason

These were jittery times politically. The government was obsessed with fears of conspiracy against the Queen. Plays were particularly suspect as a means of stirring people up, so Will and his colleagues seem to have been unusually naïve when they agreed in 1601 to a special request from the Earl of Essex to put on *Richard II*. The scene in which Richard is forced to give up the crown was considered so inflammatory that it had been cut when the play was printed. The Earl, once the Queen's favourite but now in disgrace, was indeed planning rebellion and hoped to stir up Londoners by means of the play. Either the Chamberlain's Men were sympathetic to his cause, or there had been some arm-twisting. They were brought before an examining committee but let off, perhaps on account of their patron's high office. It was a close shave for Will.

Neither one thing nor the other?

In the years in which he was creating his great tragedies Will also produced some plays that are difficult to categorise: notably *Troilus and Cressida*, *Measure for Measure* and *All's Well That Ends Well*. From their bitter, uncertain tone they are sometimes called his 'problem plays'. Though not tragedies – *Measure for Measure* and *All's Well* have conventionally happy endings – they have none of the happy spirit of the earlier comedies.

The king's a beggar, now the play is done.

All's Well that Ends Well, Act V scene 3

The plays in brief
Troilus and Cressida
1601~1602

Troilus and Cressida takes a wry look at the ancient world's most heroic story: the Trojan War, in which valiant Greeks battled valiant Trojans to repossess Helen, the most beautiful woman in the world, who had been snatched from her Greek husband by a Trojan prince.

The story of Troilus and faithless Cressida, a very minor incident in the war, was the subject of a bitter-sweet poem by Geoffrey Chaucer (c.1343–1400) which certainly influenced Will. But, whereas Chaucer's heroine (he calls her Cryseide) is a tender figure who tries to be true, Will gives the story a much sourer flavour. After nine years' fighting, Greeks and Trojans are locked in a struggle they no longer believe in. The Trojans bicker over whether to hand Helen back; the Greeks squabble amongst themselves. There is nothing heroic in war, or in love.

Cressida's character is an ambiguous one. She can be a schemer or a helpless pawn, according to the actor's interpretation. Despite her vows Troilus soon finds her in someone else's arms. The cynical Greek, Thersites, sums it up:

Lechery, lechery; still wars and lechery: nothing else holds fashion.

Measure for Measure
1603~1604

Measure for Measure, coming so soon after *Troilus*, does make one think that something in Will's life was leaving a bad taste in his mouth. It is a play of sordid motives, its gallows humour is intentionally coarse and its plot is hard for modern audiences to stomach. A heroine who declares (to a man who will spare her brother's life in exchange for sex with her) 'More than our brother is our chastity' is not going to win 21st-century hearts. However, she is a novice nun, and by the moral code of the 1600s she is taking the only possible line (for a woman) in an agonising dilemma.

The plot is an exposure of hypocrisy. (The over-zealous righteousness of the Puritans may have been in Will's sights here.) Due to an enforced absence, the Duke of Vienna has entrusted the running of the city to the incorruptible magistrate Angelo. Angelo immediately has all the brothels shut and announces that the laws on sexual misconduct will be strictly enforced. As a result, Isabella's brother Claudio is to be put to death for getting his betrothed pregnant before marriage. Isabella begs Angelo for a reprieve, which he refuses on principle. But then he is overcome by an uncharacteristic and frantic desire for her, and proposes the infamous deal.

However, the Duke has not really gone away. Disguised as a friar, he is keeping an eye on Angelo's moral crusade. He admits to a companion that he has been too lax with his subjects, but prefers that Angelo should get the flak for reinstating laws that he himself promoted but has let slip. We must blame the plot (which Will has lifted from the same collection of Italian tales that gave him *Othello*) for getting the Duke into such a dubious moral position.

The Duke is an enigmatic figure, always observing others and pulling strings to control their destinies. He contrives the scheme that traps Angelo: Isabella pretends to accept Angelo's proposition, but Angelo's own fiancée (whom he has unfairly jilted) goes instead, disguised by the dark, to fulfil Isabella's role. Then the Duke re-enters the city in his own person, calls everyone to account, rewards the good and punishes the bad. If Will meant the Duke to serve as the embodiment of divine justice, he has run into problems with some of his behaviour. He falsely and repeatedly tells the distraught Isabella that her brother has been executed, for no better reason than that it will be nice for her to learn later that he hasn't. Let's blame the plot again – but the play remains a puzzler.

Shakespeare myth no. 7

Shakespeare couldn't spell.

Nor could anyone else at the time – by modern standards – because there was no such thing then as 'spelling', in the sense of the fixed rules that it is now such a slog to learn at school. In Shakespeare's day you could spell a word in any way you liked, provided it was recognisable. People wrote the same word differently on different occasions, and sometimes even on the same page. Printers thought nothing of adding an unnecessary 'e' to the end of a word if it would help to fill the line.

Proper names were no exception. Shakespeare signed his name 'Shaksper', 'Shakspere' and 'Shakspeare'. The only words we have that are undoubtedly in his own handwriting are his signatures, so it is from these that he has been marked down in the spelling test.

You taught me language; and my profit on't
Is, I know how to curse.

The Tempest, Act I scene 2

143

The plays in brief
All's Well that Ends Well
1604~1605

All's Well that Ends Well, again based on an Italian story, shows how comedy can be thrown off balance when characters to whom Will has given the breath of real life are put through the motions of an amoral fairytale.

It begins on a promising note. A physician's daughter, Helena, cures a sick king when all his doctors have failed. For her reward, she may choose any among his courtiers as her husband. She is in love with Bertram and chooses him. He replies that he doesn't love her, didn't ask for her and won't marry her – quite an honest answer in the circumstances, though he makes it very ungraciously. The king won't accept it and he is forced to marry Helena.

Bertram leaves immediately for foreign lands, sending word that he will never acknowledge Helena as his wife unless she gets from his finger a ring which he never takes off, and conceives a child by him – which he'll make sure can never happen. The rest of the complicated plot is concerned with getting these impossible conditions fulfilled so that at the close of the play the two can be sent off to live happily together ever after.

Poor Bertram never stands a chance of gaining the audience's sympathy, since he is made to behave so shoddily throughout; and Helena, remorselessly hunting her man down, is not much more appealing. Like *Measure for Measure*, *All's Well* depends on the 'bed-partner switch', a popular ploy in folk stories, but its implication – that when it comes to sex, whether you've got the partner you think you have makes no odds – is not so digestible in romantic comedy.

All's Well that Ends Well is certainly well titled – things weren't looking too good up to that point!

All yet seems well; and if it end
so meet,[1]
The bitter past, more welcome is
the sweet.

Act V scene 3

1. *meet: fittingly, appropriately.*

The plays in brief
Timon of Athens
1605~1608

Timon, though officially a tragedy, is sometimes included amongst the problem plays. It has never been a popular one. The text is muddled in places, suggesting that it may have been left unfinished or part-written by someone else. It is a sour tale of a rich man whose main joy in life is showering his wealth on others. He accepts their assurances of undying gratitude at face value, but when his funds run out his friends cold-shoulder him.

There is an echo of *King Lear* here, though Timon does not achieve Lear's final serene abandonment of all claims on life. Instead he becomes a virulent cynic, living in a cave and shunning everyone. While digging for roots to eat, he finds a hoard of gold which brings the Athenians fawning back to him. Timon drives them away with curses. He will only use the gold to do Athens harm, giving it to the soldiers of an attacking army.

One of these soldiers later finds Timon's tomb in the woods. In defeated Athens he reports its inscription to his conquering general:

Here lie I, Timon, who, alive, all living men did hate.
Pass by, and curse thy fill; but pass and stay not here thy gait.

A bitter ending.

I should fear those that dance

before me now

Would one day stamp upon me:

't has been done;

Men shut their doors against a

setting sun.

Act I scene 2

Blackfriars theatre
(see page 151)

A stage where every man must play a part

The Merchant of Venice, *Act I scene 1*

CHAPTER EIGHT

THE KING'S MEN

 n 1603 the plague returned to London. The slums of Southwark were particularly badly hit. In Will's parish more than 2,500 people died in 6 months. This must have been one of the reasons behind his move back into the city, to a much cleaner, more respectable neighbourhood. For the next few years he was living at the corner of Silver Street and Mugwell Street in Cripplegate – an area just outside the city wall, on the site of the present-day Barbican Centre. This is the only London address of his that's known.

He lodged with a maker of theatrical headdresses (a specialist craft that suggests a working link with the players' company) called Mountjoy. We know this from a 1612 court case involving Mountjoy, in which Will was called as a witness. The dispute concerned Mountjoy's failure to pay in full the money promised eight years before as his daughter's dowry. Court records report Will as saying he had known the Mountjoy family 'as he now remembrethe for the space of tenne yeres or thereabouts', and that while living with them he had helped to arrange the daughter's marriage, though his memory of the amount of dowry agreed was very vague. Possibly he was being deliberately forgetful for the sake of his former landlord. The case reveals that by 1612 he was no longer with the Mountjoys. It describes him as being then 'of Stratford upon Avon'.

Under new management

Also in 1603, England's new monarch, James I, proved even keener on plays than Elizabeth. He took the Chamberlain's Men under his wing, and renamed them the King's Men. Will was now in theory a member of the royal household and wore the royal livery on official occasions. The Master of the Great Wardrobe issued him with 4½ yards (4.15 m) of scarlet woollen cloth to get it made.

There was a new fashion in plays, too. An indoor theatre at Blackfriars, in the City, was now in competition with open-air playhouses like the Globe. It was smaller and more intimate, and attracted a sophisticated city audience who followed the tastes of the new court. The king loved masques. These were a stylised mixture of acting, music and dance with very elaborate costumes and stage effects. The courtiers themselves loved to dress up and dance in them.

Quite an evening

Royal masques were not always stately. When James I's brother-in-law, King Christian IV of Denmark, visited England, he was entertained after dinner with a masque depicting the Queen of Sheba's visit to King Solomon.

According to the eyewitness account of Sir John Harington, the Queen of Sheba was so drunk that she tripped over a step and landed – together with a tray of wine, cream, jellies and cakes she was carrying – right in the Danish royal lap. After some mopping up, King Christian rose to dance with her, but was unable to stand and had to be carried out to an inner chamber. However, the witness reports, 'The show went forward and most of the presenters went backward or fell down, wine did so occupy their upper chambers.'

The character of Charity performed her part well enough, but her companions Faith and Hope were found 'sick and spewing in the lower hall'.

Masque costumes

By royal command

Royal personages did not go to the theatre; the players came to them. In Elizabeth's time the Chamberlain's Men had played at court 32 times. Under James the King's Men did 177 court performances, more than all their rival companies put together. Will's plays were still the top favourites, but he was competing now with a new generation of playwrights who catered to the new taste for indoor plays with music, dance and magical effects.

In his last plays he used the fantasy elements of the masques to create other-worldly worlds, where impossible reconciliations and blessings are brought about, where dreams become reality – or is everything a dream?

We are such stuff
As dreams are made on, and our
little life
Is rounded with a sleep.

The Tempest, Act IV scene 1

Pericles, Prince of Tyre
1607~1608

The earliest of Will's 'magical' plays is based on an ancient Greek tale about the perils and hardships of a wandering hero. Will knew it in a medieval retelling by the poet John Gower. The play is quite up-front about being nothing but an old tale meant to entertain. Gower himself introduces the action, and bobs up from time to time between scenes to help the story on, sometimes with characters miming a scene as he speaks. This is clumsy stagecraft and most critics doubt that Will wrote the first two acts, which may be by a minor playwright called George Wilkins.

The play's elaborate plot moves through many years and many places, telling of the wanderings and sufferings of Pericles, who loses both his wife and his daughter, believes them dead, but is reunited with them in wondrous circumstances and with divine help. These themes of death, reawakening and reunion are a constant thread in the late plays.

The plays in brief
Coriolanus
1608~1609

Will's last tragedy is a stark drama of a man destroyed through arrogance. The Roman military leader Coriolanus is a man of principle according to his own inflexible standards. He curries favour with no-one, telling a Roman mob rioting for food that they are curs and should be hanged. He wins a great victory over the Volscians[1] and is made consul,[2] but the humble address to the people that this honour entails sticks in his throat. His popularity soon plummets and he is banished.

Declaring that Rome doesn't deserve him, he joins the Volscians in attacking Rome, spurning those who plead for him to show mercy. Then, in impassioned speeches that are the highlight of the play, his mother, wife and young son beg him to relent. The ties of family are too much and he yields, though sensing it will spell disaster for him. The Volscians, furious at what they see as treachery, crowd round him and knife him to death.

1. a people who lived to the south of Rome and spoke a language related to Latin.
2. The Romans elected two consuls each year. They were the joint head of state of the republic.

Coriolanus is not a play that moves a modern audience to tears. Its characters' Roman values are uncongenial to us:

> From face to foot
> He was a thing of blood, whose every motion
> Was timed with dying cries,

a character reports admiringly of Coriolanus's battle style, and his attitude to democratic rights makes one's hair stand on end. But these are ancient Roman views, not Will's. As with all his plays, his attitude seems to be: 'Here is a drama – see what you make of it.'

Like a dull actor now,
I have forgot my part, and I
am out,
Even to a full disgrace.

Act V scene 3

The sonnets: Shakespeare's great conundrum

In 1609 Shakespeare published a collection of 154 private poems of great feeling, written in the sonnet form (a poem with 14 lines of 5 stresses and a fixed pattern of rhymes). He seems to have written them over a number of years. Francis Meres had already mentioned in 1598 his 'sugared sonnets [this was a compliment] among his private friends'. Their very personal tone confirms that originally they were only meant to be seen by friends.

The sonnets are written with such intensity that it's difficult to believe that the 'I' who expresses the love, joy, doubt, jealousy and despair they contain is not Shakespeare himself. Some are addressed to a 'fair youth' and some to a 'dark lady.' Who were these people he says he loved so much? We're still guessing. The printed edition is dedicated to 'Mr W. H.' who is described as their 'only begetter', though it's not clear whether that is Shakespeare's dedication or the publisher's. Mr W. H. has not been identified convincingly.

The plays in brief
The Winter's Tale
1609~1611

The title suggests a fairytale told by the fireside, a 'nothing' to while away the time. Its plot almost beats *Pericles* for fantasy but the play has real substance. Its first half is sombre enough. King Leontes of Sicily is overwhelmed by the irrational conviction that his wife Hermione is unfaithful. He has her imprisoned and her young son taken from her, and sends messengers to the oracle at Delphi to confirm her guilt. When Hermione gives birth to a daughter in prison, Leontes has the baby exposed to die, on the grounds that it is a bastard.

Hermione is standing trial for adultery when the oracle's answer is brought back: Hermione is chaste,

Leontes a jealous tyrant, his innocent babe truly begotten, and the king shall live without an heir if that which is lost be not found.

Leontes refuses at first to believe this verdict, but when his son dies suddenly he accepts that this is his punishment from the gods. He repents too late – Hermione has died of grief. Bereft of wife and children, Leontes vows to spend a lifetime mourning them.

The events of the second half occur in a sunnier place and time. Time himself steps on stage to explain the fairytale adjustments that the passage of 16 years has made to the story, and to hint that there is more to come :

> *but let Time's news*
> *Be known when 'tis brought forth.*

In the bringing forth we meet Perdita, an enchanting shepherdess who is wooed by the prince of Bohemia's son. His father rages against such a mismatch, but it is a fairytale cloud soon blown away. Perdita[1] proves to be that abandoned baby, who of course was saved from death. Past sadness melts away; parents and children are reunited and Leontes' long dead wife is restored to him (though he has done little to deserve it). For those who don't know the story it would be a pity to reveal how this happens, since it works so miraculously on stage. You have to see it. The healing passage of time brings a blessing to everyone, deserved or undeserved.

Exit, pursued by a bear.

Act III scene 3[2]

1. *Her name means 'lost' in Latin.*
2. *Is this the greatest stage direction ever? It has been suggested that a real bear might have been borrowed from the nearby bear-baiting ring.*

The plays in brief
Cymbeline
1610~1611

Cymbeline owes a lot to the new taste for masque-like staging and intricate artificial plot-lines. It's impossible to put the plot in a nutshell, but in essentials it tells of a falsely accused princess, Imogen, who disguises herself as a boy to seek reconciliation with her estranged husband, Posthumus. En route she is threatened with assassination, loses her way, is sheltered by woodsmen (two of whom are, unknown to her, her long-lost brothers), swallows a death-draught sent by her wicked stepmother, and recovers to find a headless corpse by her side, wearing her husband's clothes. And we are only halfway through Act IV!

There is much more to come, including a dream sequence in which the god Jupiter is wound down onto the stage astride an eagle, to the accompaniment of lightning and thunderbolts, in true masque fashion.

If you think this sounds more like a pantomime than a serious play, you're not allowing for Shakespeare's skill in creating something that is more than the sum of its parts. In the final scene he brings the main characters together at the court of King Cymbeline[1] and with a series

1. *loosely based on the ancient British king Cunobelinus.*

of breathtaking disclosures transforms the lives of every one of them. No fewer than nine confessions, revelations or recognitions follow thick and fast — all potentially ludicrous, but transformed by the characters' very human responses into a swell of happiness that is genuinely moving.

> *Hang there like fruit, my soul,*
> *Till the tree die,*

says Posthumus, as his restored wife flings her arms around his neck. All divisions — between husband and wife, father and children, separated friends and warring nations — are healed. In the words of the soothsayer who interprets the will of the gods:

> *The fingers of the powers above do tune*
> *The harmony of this peace.*

Is there no way for men to be,
but women
Must be half-workers?

Act II scene 5

The Tempest
1610~1611

The plot of this play seems to be Will's own invention – the only one that is. It opens with a spectacular storm at sea, in which Antonio, the unlawful Duke of Milan, together with Alonso, King of Naples, his brother Sebastian and his son Ferdinand, are cast ashore on a mysterious island. They are unaware that the storm has been magically created by Antonio's brother Prospero, the rightful Duke. The island is his and he commands its spirits, including Ariel, an airy being, and the brutish Caliban.

Prospero tells his daughter Miranda the reason for the storm. Twelve years ago his brother, whom he had entrusted with his dukedom in order to study, had conspired with Alonso to seize it, and had set Prospero and Miranda adrift at sea. Prospero had his books of magic which a loyal retainer had smuggled into the boat. He has raised the storm to bring his enemies into his sphere of power. He means to deal with them.

This could have developed into a revenge tragedy, but Will means to show that forgiveness is a nobler satisfaction than revenge. Prospero's enchantments confuse his island visitors to the point where he has them literally spellbound. Then he releases them:

The sole drift of my purpose doth extend
Not a frown further. Go release them, Ariel:
My charms I'll break, their senses I'll restore
And they shall be themselves.

At the end of the play Prospero's authority is not only physically but spiritually transforming. Base characters become radiant, as Miranda exclaims on first seeing them:

> *O wonder!*
> *How many goodly creatures are there here!*
> *How beauteous mankind is! O brave new*
> *world,*
> *That has such creatures in't.*

Full fathom five[1] thy father lies;
Of his bones are coral made;
Those are pearls that were
his eyes;
Nothing of him that doth fade,
But doth suffer a sea-change
Into something rich and strange.

Act I scene 2

---

1. *Full fathom five: at a depth of 30 ft (9.14 m).*

The Tempest is Will's last solo work. It's tempting to see its tale of a magician who quits the enchanted world he has created as a reflection of Will's own feeling that it's time to bow out. He was in his late forties, which was quite an age in those days, and it seems he was slackening off.

He had the means to retire, and a house waiting for him. A Stratford lawyer and his family had been living at New Place, but in May 1611 the lawyer bought a house of his own – which suggests that Will had told him he would soon need the space for himself. If Will was already in Stratford by 1611 he must have been back and forth to London quite a bit. He was still working. His last plays, *Henry VIII* (1613) and *The Two Noble Kinsmen* (1613–1614, a courtly tale drawn from Chaucer), were co-written with up-and-coming playwright John Fletcher, whom the King's Men were grooming to step into Shakespeare's shoes.

Whenever he made the final break, he didn't enjoy a long retirement. He died in Stratford on 23 April – St George's day – 1616, and was buried there in Holy Trinity church. His death is as unexplained as much of his life. According to Stratford gossip (reported over 40 years later), 'Shakespeare, Drayton[1] and Ben Jonson had a merry meeting and it seems drank too hard, for Shakespeare died of a fever there contracted.' Since Aubrey noted that he was a remarkably temperate drinker, we need not believe this. He may have had a couple of pints and caught a chill on the way home. Or it's suggested that he may have died of typhoid fever, which was prevalent. Or he may have had a lingering illness that had prompted his retirement. We can only guess.

Our revels now are ended; these our actors,
As I foretold you, were all spirits and
Are melted into air, into thin air.

The Tempest, Act IV scene 1

1. *Michael Drayton (1563–1631), poet and playwright.*

Shakespeare myth no. 8

In his will he showed just what he thought of his wife by leaving her his second-best bed.

This sounds like an insult. Why didn't he leave her the best bed? And why didn't he leave her anything else?

The fact is that there was no need to make special provision for Anne. Under common law she was entitled to a dower-right of one third of his estate. The best bed in a household was reserved for guests. Will and Anne would have slept in the second bed, the marital bed which had symbolic importance. It represented the permanent union of man and wife. Shakespeare may have had this in mind in mentioning it, or it may have been an heirloom from the Hathaway home in Shottery. There is no reason to think he went out of his way to snub his wife.

New Place, Shakespeare's last home

Too late!

One of the biggest 'if onlys' in world literature:

At the beginning of the 1660s, John Ward, vicar of Holy Trinity church, Stratford-upon-Avon, made a memo that he must get round to having a talk with Judith Quiney, Shakespeare's only surviving offspring (her sister Susanna had died in 1649). Judith was already pretty old for those days – over 75. He didn't get round to it, and she died in 1662. Just think what she could have told him!

There wouldn't have been so many 'probablies' in this book, for one thing...

When we are born, we cry that we are come
To this great stage of fools.

King Lear, Act IV scene 6

The end of the
first Globe (see
page 177)

 ittle fire
grows great
with little wind...

The Taming of the Shrew, *Act II scene 1*

CHAPTER NINE

AfTER SHAKESPEARE

 t the time Will died, only 18 of his plays had appeared in print, in cheap, unauthorised editions which were often full of mistakes. His friends thought something should done about this. Two of his fellow players, John Heminges and Henry Condell, collected together 36 plays and everything else they considered to be by him, in the best possible copies, and in 1623 they had them printed in folio form (the large format used for serious publications). They didn't include *Pericles*, probably because someone else had had a hand in it.

With hindsight we can see that this was a huge publishing landmark. Without Heminges's and Condell's efforts half of Will's output, including *Macbeth*, *Julius Caesar*, *As You like It*, *Twelfth Night*, *A Winter's Tale* and *The Tempest*, would have disappeared completely.

Be not afraid of greatness: some are born great, some achieve greatness, and some have greatness thrust upon 'em.

Twelfth Night, Act II scene 5

Gone missing: the plays that fell through the net

Francis Meres's 1598 list names a play called *Love's Labour's Won*. There is no trace of it today. For a long time it was thought that Meres was referring to an existing play by another title – *The Taming of the Shrew*, perhaps. But in 1953 a dealer discovered a 1603 bookseller's catalogue that listed 'marchant of vennis, taming of a shrew, loves labor lost, loves labor won'. So *Love's Labour's Won* can't have been *The Taming of the Shrew*. Maybe Will wrote a sequel to *Love's Labour's Lost*, telling what happened to its lovesick nobles once their 12 months' probation was over.

Another casualty, *Cardenio*, certainly existed. It was put on in 1613. In 1653 a bookseller listed it as being by William Shakespeare and John Fletcher (1579–1625; a playwright Will collaborated with towards the end of his career). But that particular bookseller is known to have put Will's name to things just to get a better sale. No copy has so far turned up, so we don't know what *Cardenio* was – a lost treasure, a bungled collaboration, or not by Will at all?

Times change

Fashions in plays were already changing by the time Will quit the stage. After his death he began to seem old-fashioned. Then for a time there were no plays at all. Under Cromwell's Commonwealth all the theatres were closed. By the time they reopened, with the return of Charles II in 1660, the appetite for Shakespeare had picked up, but only if the plays could be licked into better shape. It was agreed that Will had done a messy job. *Hamlet* was described as having 'an indifferent good part for a madman', and the diarist and civil servant Samuel Pepys called *A Midsummer Night's Dream* 'the most insipid ridiculous play I ever saw in my life'.

The major complaints were that Will's language was over-elaborate and full of puns, that he had too many low-class characters, he muddled tragedy with comedy and he lacked 'moral taste'. By this people meant that he allowed the wrong sort of thing to happen. For instance, Lear and Cordelia shouldn't have been allowed to die.

Setting Shakespeare straight

Dramatists set about putting things right. Nahum Tate's 1681 *King Lear* had a happy ending. Tate described finding the original *Lear* 'a heap of jewels, unstrung and unpolished; yet so dazzling in their disorder that I soon perceived I had seized a treasure.'

Restringing Will's jewels was a favourite activity of 17th- and 18th-century playwrights. They altered plots; they cut and rewrote. They saw nothing wrong with this: Will's plays had always belonged to the stage world and were fair game for rewriting. William Davenant blended *Measure for Measure* with *Much Ado about Nothing* to create *The Law against Lovers*. In Dryden's version of *Troilus and Cressida*, Cressida is faithful. Colley Cibber totally rehashed *Richard III* and managed one line so in character that even Will might might have been proud of it:

Off with his head: so much for Buckingham!

It wasn't till the 19th century that actors and managers began to trust Will's texts to do the job. The new respect that was accorded to him resulted in lavish productions. Actor-manager Charles Kean's 1859 staging of *Henry V* had a cast of 550. Elaborate stage settings required cumbersome scenery that took so long to shift that the plays had to be savagely cut.

Bardolatry

That was George Bernard Shaw's mocking term[1] for the over-reverential attitude to Shakespeare that developed in the 19th century. This grew out of the sort of Shakespeare criticism that concentrates on the plays as works of literature rather than as actors' scripts. Shakespeare's achievements were rated so miraculous, so sublime, that some people began querying how a country bumpkin, a glover's son, could have written them. Such a person might have become an actor, but a genius – never!

---

1. based on bard, a pretentious word for 'poet', and idolatry, the worship of idols.

Anti-Stratfordians

This was the beginning of the great authorship controversy. It got going in the 1850s. The argument was (and is – there are still supporters around) that the plays show such knowledge of court life, statesmanship and military strategy, and reveal such an educated mind, that only a nobleman or court insider could have written them.

So what about the fact that Will is named seven times in official records as the author of plays performed before King James? What about Francis Meres's tribute to him? And what about Heminges's and Condell's clear statement that they were publishing plays written by William Shakespeare?

Supporters of anti-Stratfordian theories, as they're called, brush this evidence aside. They each believe that their very distinguished candidate had an aristocratic distaste for anything associated with the stage, and therefore preferred to use a humble actor as his 'front man'.

There are many rival contenders; among the most favoured are:

- **philosopher and scientist Sir Francis Bacon**
- **the Earl of Oxford**
- **the Earl of Derby**
- **playwright Christopher Marlowe.**

Marlowe died in 1593 with 30 plays still to write, so the theory requires that his death must have been faked.

It's all pretty ridiculous. The anti-Stratfordians can't produce a scrap of evidence that would stand up in court. They rely on clues they think they detect in the plays. If you look for codes and anagrams, as some do, you can 'prove' whatever you like.

This red herring sprang out of concentrating on the plays as literature and ignoring the fact that they were tailored for the stage by someone with practical stagecraft – which you don't learn at court. The balance was redressed in the 20th century, very largely through a revolutionary series of studies, *Prefaces to Shakespeare* by Harley Granville

Barker, which started coming out in 1927. Granville Barker was a Shakespeare scholar, an actor and a dramatist – an ideal combination. He pioneered the idea that the plays can best be appreciated, and staged, by considering the requirements of the theatre they were written for.

A new Globe

That's an approach that Will would have understood much better than bardolatry. It led to one of the biggest Shakespearean achievements of the 20th century: the rebuilding of the Globe theatre on Bankside, close to its original site.

The first Globe burned down by accident on 29 June 1613, its thatched roof set alight by a cannon fired during a performance of *Henry VIII*.[1] Its replacement (with a tiled roof) was operational about a year later, but was closed down by the Puritans in 1642 and demolished soon after.

---

1. *There were no casualties, but it is said that one customer's breeches caught fire and had to be doused with ale.*

The present Globe on Bankside, now officially known as 'Shakespeare's Globe', was opened by the second Queen Elizabeth on 12 June 1997. Its creation was due almost entirely (be it said to Britain's shame) to the tireless campaigning of American actor and director Sam Wanamaker (1919–1993). Here you can see Will's plays done much as his company did them (as far as we can judge), and in the setting he knew. That doesn't in itself guarantee a good performance, of course. No one way of doing Shakespeare is 'right'. Will would have been the first to say that what matters is whatever works in the theatre.

Tower of London

St Saviour's Church
(now Southwark Cathedral)

The Globe

London Bridge

Bankside in Shakespeare's time

A Shakespeare Quiz

Can you spot where these quotations come from?
Do you know which characters said them?

1. Uneasy lies the head that wears a crown.

2. What's in a name? That which we call a rose
    By any other name would smell as sweet.

3. How sharper than a serpent's tooth it is
    To have a thankless child.

4. If we shadows have offended,
    Think but this, and all is mended:
    That you have but slumber'd here
    While these visions did appear.

5. This above all – to thine own self be true;
    And it must follow, as the night the day,
    Thou canst not then be false to any man.

6. The quality of mercy is not strain'd –
    It droppeth as the gentle rain from heaven
    Upon the place beneath.

1. *King Henry in* Henry IV Part II, *Act III scene 1.*
2. *Juliet in* Romeo and Juliet, *Act II scene 1.*
3. *King Lear in* King Lear, *Act I scene 4.*
4. *Puck in* A Midsummer Night's Dream, *Act V scene 1.*
5. *Polonius in* Hamlet, *Act I scene 3.*
6. *Portia in* The Merchant of Venice, *Act IV scene 1.*

Glossary

alderman A town official ranking next to the mayor.

apprentice An unpaid trainee who serves a master-craftsman for a fixed number of years in return for training.

banns Public announcements of a proposed marriage, required to be made in church on three successive Sundays, so that anyone who knew of a legal objection to the marriage could raise it.

bard Originally a Celtic term for a singer of narrative poems and, later, a 'poetic' term for a poet.

Bard, the Short for 'the Bard of Avon', a nickname for Shakespeare which was coined in the 18th century and is now often used ironically.

blank verse Unrhymed verse in iambic pentameter.

branded Burned on the skin with a permanent distinguishing mark from a hot iron; once a common punishment for minor offences.

burgess A member of the governing body of a town.

catechism The basic beliefs of Christianity set out in the form of questions and answers, which pupils had to learn.

chronicle A record of historical events.

City, the That part of London which was contained within its medieval walls; then as now, London's main commercial centre.

comedy A play which contains both noble and common characters and has a happy ending.

Commonwealth The period from the execution of Charles I in 1649 to the restoration of Charles II in

1660, during which England, Scotland and Ireland formed a Republic.

create (a role) Be the first actor to play it.

dower-right The portion of a husband's wealth which his widow is entitled to during her lifetime, by law.

ensign A low-ranking infantry officer, originally the carrier of the ensign (flag).

farthingale A framework of cane or metal hoops used to hold out women's skirts in the 16th century.

First Folio The first collected edition of Shakespeare's works, edited by John Heminges and Henry Condell and published in 1623.

folio A book made up of large sheets of paper folded in half to form two leaves. (Folding it again, into four leaves, produced a smaller 'quarto' book). Folio format was for used for important works.

iambic pentameter A verse line composed of five 'feet' (pairs of syllables) in which the second syllable is stressed, the first unstressed: in crude terms, te-TUM te-TUM te-TUM te-TUM te-TUM.

jig A short entertainment, with dance, mime and song, usually performed after the main play in 16th-century theatres.

livery A distinctive uniform worn by an important person's servants.

Lord Chamberlain The senior official of the Royal Household.

masque A dramatic entertainment of dialogue, dance and song, with scenic effects and lavish costumes, that became fashionable in the early 17th century.

messuage A portion of land containing a dwelling-house and its outbuildings.

oratory The art of public speaking.

patron An important person who agrees to use his influence to protect others, in return for their services.

Protestant A member of the Reformed Church which declared itself independent of the Roman Catholic Church in the 16th century.

Puritans English Protestants who thought that Elizabethan reform of the Church had not gone far enough and that it needed to be further 'purified'. They were noted for their moral strictness.

Roman Catholic A Christian who remains faithful to the teachings and organisation of the pre-Reformation Church, whose spiritual head is the Pope, based in Rome.

Saxon Belonging to the period in England that preceded the Norman Conquest of 1066.

scaffold A temporary wooden platform, especially one on which an execution takes place.

Stationers' Register A record book kept by the Stationers' Company of London (which regulated the publishing industry). Registering a work gave a publisher the sole right to print it.

tenement A building divided into many units for letting.

tragedy A play which shows an important personage brought low, usually because of some personal flaw.

trestle A wooden support with two legs in a V-shape at each end, used to make a temporary table or stage.

yeoman A man who owned a small estate, but did not have the rank of 'gentleman'.

A Shakespeare timeline

Note: Dates of plays are only approximate.

1564 Playwright Christopher Marlowe born. William, son of John and Mary Shakespeare, baptised April 26 at Holy Trinity Church, Stratford-upon-Avon.

1567 Actor-manager Richard Burbage born.

1569 John Shakespeare appointed town bailiff.

1572 Playwright Ben Jonson born.

1576 James Burbage opens The Theatre in Shoreditch, London.

1577 The Curtain theatre opens in Shoreditch.

1582 27 November: Shakespeare marries Anne Hathaway.

1583 26 May: Their daughter Susanna is christened.

1585 2 February: Their twins Hamnet and Judith are christened.

1587 Mary, Queen of Scots is executed. The Rose theatre is built on Bankside.

1588 Defeat of Spanish Armada. Marlowe's *Dr Faustus* first performed.

?late 1580s Shakespeare moves to London.

1589–1590 *The Two Gentlemen of Verona*

1590 Marlowe's *Jew of Malta* first performed.

c.1590 *The Taming of the Shrew*

1590–1592 *Henry VI Parts I, II and III*

1591–1594 *A Comedy of Errors*

1592 Thomas Kyd's *Spanish Tragedy* published. Robert Greene's pamphlet *A Groatsworth of Wit* contains earliest known reference to Shakespeare as an upstart young dramatist.

c.1592–1593 *Titus Andronicus*

1592–1593 *Richard III*

1593 Plague shuts theatres from February 1593 until June 1594. *Venus and Adonis* published. Christopher Marlowe is murdered.

1594 *The Rape of Lucrece* is recorded in the Stationers' Register, 9 May. The Chamberlain's Men formed; Shakespeare is a member. Thomas Kyd dies.

1594–1595 *Love's Labour's Lost, Richard II*

1595 December: Shakespeare is named among players paid for performing before Queen Elizabeth.

1595–1596 *Romeo and Juliet, A Midsummer Night's Dream*

1595–1597 *King John*

1596 *Henry IV Part I.* Shakespeare's son Hamnet is buried at Stratford, 11 August. Coat of arms granted to John Shakespeare, 20 October.

1596–1597 *The Merchant of Venice*

1597 4 May: Shakespeare buys New Place, Stratford.

1597–1598 *The Merry Wives of Windsor*

1598 *Henry IV Part II.* Francis Meres praises Shakespeare in *Palladis Tamia: Wits* [sic] *Treasury.* December: demolition of The Theatre.

1598–1599 *Much Ado about Nothing*

1599 Shakespeare named as a shareholder in the Globe theatre, 21 February. Chamberlain's Men move to the newly built Globe. Thomas Platter of Basel describes a performance of *Julius Caesar* at the Globe. *Henry V* performed.

c.1600 *Hamlet*

1600 *As You Like It.* Fortune theatre built by Edward Alleyn. August 23: *Henry IV Part II* entered in the

Stationers' Register under Shakespeare's name – the first mention of his name in the Register.

1601 Robert Devereux, Earl of Essex leads a revolt against Queen Elizabeth and is executed. John Shakespeare is buried at Holy Trinity Church, Stratford, 8 September.

1601–1602 *Twelfth Night, Troilus and Cressida*

1602 1 May: Shakespeare pays £320 for 107 acres of farmland near Stratford. 28 September: Buys ¼ acre of land and a cottage in Chapel Lane, Stratford.

1603 Queen Elizabeth I dies, 24 March. James I (= James VI of Scotland) arrives in London. 19 May: Royal patent renames the Lord Chamberlain's Men as the King's Men.

1603–1604 *Measure for Measure, Othello*

1604–1605 *All's Well That Ends Well.* During this winter, The Kings Men's 11 performances at court include 7 plays by Shakespeare.

1605 *King Lear.* Shakespeare invests £440 in Stratford tithes, 24 July. Gunpowder Plot foiled, 5 November.

1605–1608 *Timon of Athens*

1606 *Macbeth*

1606–1607 *Antony and Cleopatra*

1607 5 June: Shakespeare's elder daughter Susanna marries Dr John Hall at Holy Trinity, Stratford.

1607–1608 *Pericles*

1608 Shakespeare's mother dies.

1608–1609 *Coriolanus*

1609 20 May: Shakespeare's **Sonnets** entered in Stationers' Register. Winter: performances at Blackfriars begin.

1609–1611 *The Winter's Tale*

1610–1611 *Cymbeline, The Tempest*

1613 *Henry VIII.* 29 June: The Globe theatre burns down during a performance of *Henry VIII*.

c.1613 *Cardenio*, written with John Fletcher.

1613–1614 *The Two Noble Kinsmen*, written with John Fletcher.

1614 Rebuilt Globe reopens.

1616 25 January: Shakespeare's will is drawn up. 10 February: Shakespeare's younger daughter, Judith, marries Thomas Quiney. 25 March: Shakespeare revises his will. 23 April: Shakespeare dies.

1623 August: Shakespeare's wife Anne dies. 8 November: First Folio published.

1642 The second Globe theatre is closed under the Commomwealth movement to abolish theatrical performances.

c.1644 The Globe is demolished.

1649 11 July: Susanna Hall, née Shakespeare, dies.

1662 9 February: Judith Quiney, née Shakespeare, is buried.

1997 A replica of the Globe theatre opens on Bankside, near the original site.

Index

Very Peculiar Histories™

Ancient Egypt
Mummy Myth and Magic
Jim Pipe
ISBN: 978-1-906714-92-5

The Blitz
David Arscott
ISBN: 978-1-907184-18-5

Brighton
David Arscott
ISBN: 978-1-906714-89-5

Castles
Jacqueline Morley
ISBN: 978-1-907184-48-2

Charles Dickens
Fiona Macdonald
ISBN: 978-1-908177-15-5

Christmas
Fiona Macdonald
ISBN: 978-1-907184-50-5

Global Warming
Ian Graham
ISBN: 978-1-907184-51-2

Golf
David Arscott
ISBN: 978-1-907184-75-8

Great Britons
Ian Graham
ISBN: 978-1-907184-59-8

Ireland
Jim Pipe
ISBN: 978-1-905638-98-7

Kings & Queens
Antony Mason
ISBN: 978-1-906714-77-2

London
Jim Pipe
ISBN: 978-1-907184-26-0

The Olympics
David Arscott
ISBN: 978-1-907184-78-9

Queen Elizabeth II
David Arscott
ISBN: 978-1-908177-50-6

Rations
David Arscott
ISBN: 978-1-907184-25-3

Royal Weddings
Fiona Macdonald
ISBN: 978-1-907184-84-0

Scotland
Fiona Macdonald

**Vol. 1: From ancient times
to Robert the Bruce**
ISBN: 978-1-906370-91-6

**Vol. 2: From the Stewarts
to modern Scotland**
ISBN: 978-1-906714-79-6

Titanic
Jim Pipe
ISBN: 978-1-907184-87-1

The Tudors
Jim Pipe
ISBN: 978-1-907184-58-1

Vampires
Fiona Macdonald
ISBN: 978-1-907184-39-0

Victorian Servants
Fiona Macdonald
ISBN: 978-1-907184-49-9

Wales
Rupert Matthews
ISBN: 978-1-907184-19-2

Whisky
Fiona Macdonald
ISBN: 978-1-907184-76-5

The World Cup
David Arscott
ISBN: 978-1-907184-38-3

World War One
Jim Pipe
ISBN: 978-1-908177-00-1

Yorkshire
John Malam
ISBN: 978-1-907184-57-4

Heroes, Gods and Monsters

Heroes, Gods and
Monsters of
**Ancient Greek
Mythology**
Michael Ford
ISBN: 978-1-906370-92-3

Heroes, Gods and
Monsters of
**Celtic
Mythology**
Fiona Macdonald
ISBN: 978-1-905638-97-0